55 Years
On the Footplate

Reminiscences of the Southern at Bournemouth

by
Stan Symes

THE OAKWOOD PRESS

© Oakwood Press & Stan Symes 1995

British Library Cataloguing in Publication Data
A Record for this book is available from the British Library
ISBN 0 85361 484 9

Typeset by Oakwood Graphics.

Printed by Henry Ling Limited, The Dorset Press, Dorchester.

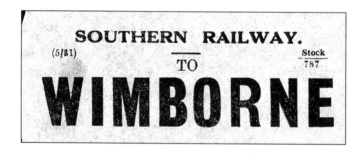

Published by
The Oakwood Press
P.O. Box 122, Headington, Oxford OX3 8LU

Contents

These black metal boxes were widely used by train crews. They were made by Dukes of Grimsby.

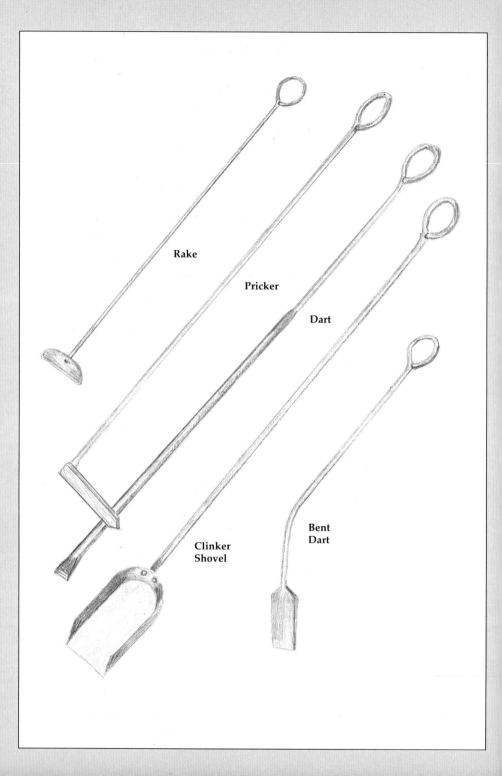

Rake

Pricker

Dart

Clinker
Shovel

Bent
Dart

Chapter One

Cleaning Days

With World War II rapidly approaching I was working for a small Dairy Company when, one day, I met a friend of the family, Harry Fox who was a driver at Dorchester. He asked me if I would consider a job on the Southern Railway starting off as an engine cleaner and eventually working up to train driver. If so he would make enquiries to that end. Whilst I had no thoughts in that direction I was, in fact, very disenchanted with my job as a milkman, its early start at around 4.30 am and its 365 days a year roster, so I said I would welcome a change.

In due course I had to go down to the Engine Shed at Beechy Road, Bournemouth to see the chief clerk to make out a form to apply for a vacancy. On completing it, I was informed that as soon as an appointment could be arranged I would have to travel up to Southampton to see the Doctor appointed by the railway company to carry out medical examinations to ensure that the high standards required in physical fitness, eyesight and colour vision were met.

During early August 1939, in company with two other young men, Doug Scott and Stan Lapping, I went by train up to Southampton and we were all successful in passing the Doctor's examination. Then at 6.00 am on Monday 28th August we all started our first day as temporary engine cleaners.

We reported for duty and were taken under the wing of the cleaner foreman, Tom Glassey, a small man but one respected by all. He asked us our ages; Doug was 17, Stan and I were 16 but my birthday was before his so our seniority was as follows, Doug first, then me, with Stan last. Seniority was in order of starting date but if more than one started on the same date then age was used to establish it. Seniority was all important because it affected your whole railway career and was used to determine the order in which cleaners were booked out as firemen, then promotion to firemen as a vacancy occurred, for promotion in the different links and eventually promotion to driver.

Tom briefly explained our duties and led us out, in company with the rest of the cleaners, to clean our first locomotive, 'King Arthur' class No. 785. This was the first time I had been close to an engine and it seemed enormous to me, towering above us but it had to be cleaned for the first train from Bournemouth West to Waterloo at 7.35 am. We were soon swarming all over it and in a very short time it had been cleaned, with the paintwork shining in its beautiful Southern Railway malachite green, its brass and copper gleaming and its steelwork scoured with emery cloth.

No sooner had we completed this task than we were put to work on 'Schools' class No. 926 *Repton* to repeat the process to ready it for the 8.35 am from Bournemouth West.

Teamwork under Tom's watchful eye made a rapid transformation to the appearance and it was soon ready for service. 'Right', said Tom, 'Off you go to breakfast' and we all made a beeline for the cleaners' cabin for our 20 minute break. Tom was always generous in his time allowance and when he arrived to stir us into action his words were always, 'Right, let's have you!' He led the way to the far end of the Engine Shed where he kept his supply of cleaning cloths, buckets, mineral oil, emery cloth, brick dust and petroleum jelly used for engine cleaning. He would divide the cleaners up into gangs of four, hand them a bucket of cleaning materials, give them the number of the engine to be cleaned and walk around to make sure we were not 'skiving' and were doing the job to his satisfaction.

We had a variety of locomotives at Bournemouth, ranging from 0-4-0 tank locos to 'King Arthur' 4-6-0 tender locos. The 0-4-0s were nicknamed 'Bugs', the 'M7' 0-4-4 tanks were called motor tanks because they were used on push and pull trains. We had small hoppers, large hoppers, 'T9s', goods locomotives Nos. 521-524, Black Motors, 'Qs', 'Woolies', Adams tanks and 'Schools' class Nos. 924 to 933 which were our main line passenger engines used on express trains. Six of these engines were allocated to the main line link, each locomotive being shared by two sets of men. Great pride was taken in them because of this arrangement and they were kept spotlessly clean on the footplate with the fire irons always in good order as were the lamps, coal shovel, spanners etc. Around this time the large enamel advertising boards were being replaced by posters and the firemen would try to get hold of one to place on the tender beneath the coal to give a good surface to shovel coal forward when necessary at the end of the outward journey, in readiness for the return journey.

These six locomotives were also allocated to individual cleaners over 18 years old, who would start work at midnight and clean the engine during the night in readiness for the next day's work. Everything was cleaned, the paintwork, wheels, footframings etc., were wiped over with mineral oil, then polished with a dry cloth. The boiler was greased with petroleum jelly to make it shine and then the whistle, name plates as well as all the copper pipes were polished with finely ground brick dust to produce a brilliant shine. Finally, the steelwork was scoured with emery cloth. This included buffers, smokebox door ring, front hand rail, lamp brackets as well as parts of the valve gear. The tenders of these engines were cleaned by a gang of four cleaners who went round them in turn cleaning the paintwork, the frames, axleboxes etc. The finish of these locos was far superior to the paint applied during and after the war, with much less effort needed to obtain the beautiful appearance produced by dedicated men.

At the end of my first week all the cleaners were told to report for duty on Sunday 3rd September, which was unprecedented at that time. Sunday work for cleaners was, in fact, unheard of.

At 11.00 am that morning war was declared and immediately preparations were made to make the shed safer in the event of an air raid. All windows were taped to minimise the risk of injuries from flying glass. Sand bags were filled and placed around the running foreman's office which was in a very exposed position. Everyone was full of apprehension, expecting air raids at any time but nothing happened. Life was full of little irritations such as no lights in the streets, very little light in the Engine Shed, which took a while to get used to because of such obstacles as water hydrants, cleaning steps, hose pipes and all the stacks of firebars, firebricks, sleepers for firelighting that were part and parcel of a locomotive depot.

My cleaning days were happy ones and I formed a firm friendship with Doug Scott with whom I always worked, in company with Stan Lapping and Bernard Wharton.

One day Tom Glassey gave us a bucket of cleaning materials and said, 'There you are, go and clean half hundred' meaning 'M7' class tank engine No. 50, but as a joke we went to 'B4' class No. 100 drawing a line down the centre of the smokebox and cab and proceeded to clean one side only which did not take long owing to its very small size.

We returned to Tom's 'Den' and he was amazed that we had taken such a short time, so off he went to inspect our work but he returned fuming saying, 'Idiots, I meant both sides of 50 not one side of 100, now you can go and finish off 100 and then you can clean 50', adding as an afterthought, 'both sides'.

He had a good sense of humour but I noticed that he avoided giving us No. 50 to clean for a long time afterwards.

He gave me the job every morning to walk up to the station to place a '381 Duty' board on the front of the 8.40 am to Waterloo (which started from Weymouth at 7.35 am) so that it was clean for this important train. As cleaners were not normally allowed to go to the station I used to obtain various items for the others on duty such as chocolate, sweets, cigarette and fruit which I purchased from the buffet trolley positioned on the up platform. One day I could not get a jaffa orange that one cleaner had asked for so I went out of the station to purchase it at a nearby greengrocer's, passing the chief clerk on his way to the office. He nodded a curt 'Good Morning' to me and went on his way, but when I returned to the Shed Tom told me to go and report to him.

He was well known for his arrogant sarcasm and he gave me a ticking off for leaving railway premises, telling me that in future I must see Mr Steele, the shed master, to obtain such permission.

Later on that morning Tom told me that I was required by the chief clerk and when I arrived at his window he handed me a bottle with a prescription, plus a sixpence, telling me to go to the Chemist to get it for him. I then asked to see Mr Steele to which he said, 'What do you want to see him for?', to which I replied 'To ask permission to leave the railway premises'. I beat a hasty retreat because I am sure he would have exploded had I not done so and went to purchase his medicine. I was dreading his reaction when I returned, but he took the bottle with a mumbled 'Thank you' and he could not supress a slightly amused expression which showed me he was human after all, not that many would have believed it.

On Christmas Eve 1939 I got my first firing turn on engine No. 239 which was an 0-6-0T yard shunter along with driver George Graysmark on the late shift at Bournemouth Central Goods Yard. This locomotive was only fitted with a hand brake which the fireman used and it proved to be a very busy turn of duty. I had to do the normal firing duties as best I could in between shunting, while George used the regulator and reverser to make the various movements required. Under his watchful eye I made a reasonably good job of it, but I will admit I was thankful when we had finished shunting and took the engine to Shed, where I had to throw out the fire as it was not required on Christmas Day.

The previous week I had been informed that the quota for cleaners was now 40. Unfortunately I was No. 41 and I was given the choice of being stood off or agreeing to go to Basingstoke on loan as they were short of cleaners there.

Not wanting to break my service, I decided to go and on 1st January, 1940 I was sent there with Stan Lapping, who was junior to me, being sent to Faversham, so our quartet was broken up for the time being.

I reported to the Shed Master on arrival, being then directed to lodgings that they had found for me, with Jim Oliver, the boilerwasher at the Shed who had the dubious nickname of 'Twister'. Not, I hasten to add, because of his character but because of the name of Oliver, as in Oliver Twist.

I enjoyed my stay with Jim and his family but did not like being away from home, so I returned there every week-end, travelling down on Saturday afternoon and returning on Sunday evening, to be on time for an 8.00 am start on Monday.

We worked a six day week with eight hour shifts, being under the charge of the Shed engineman as there was neither running foreman nor cleaner foreman at Basingstoke at that time. Several other cleaners came there at the same time, one from Eastleigh, one from the Isle of Wight and one from Guildford. Three others started work on the day I arrived so we were all new to the depot and soon got to know each other well, going out to the cinema or a show if we could afford it in the evenings.

The winter of 1939-40 was a very cold one with heavy snowfalls. That, coupled with Basingstoke station's high and exposed position, convinced me that it was the coldest place on earth, a view that ensuing years confirmed in my mind, it being so draughty there.

Bob Bruce and I, both cleaners, were given the job of keeping the fires going in the braziers that were used to prevent the water columns from freezing up. This entailed walking from Barton Mill sidings through the station then on as far as the West Yard. We had constantly to add coal to each in turn, nine braziers in all, often finding that those at each extreme had burnt out, making it necessary to re-light them with a couple of firelighters that we carried with us. We had to trudge through snow often up and over our knees, soaking our legs and feet, which took a lot of sticking but we made light of it as we liked each other's company. Also we were free to do the job without having someone watching over us. This went on for two weeks before there was a thaw but we suffered no ill effects from our daily soakings. Then it was back to our cleaning duties.

I had a lot of firing turns during my stay there, mostly shunting, of course, and I found that the drivers there were mostly easy going men, ready and willing to teach a young lad the art of firing.

There was one exception, who shall be nameless for obvious reasons, but he was the most miserable man it has been my misfortune to work with. He would not tell you what to do but would say, 'Don't you think you ought to be doing something?' On looking at the state of the boiler, fire etc., when you decided what to do it was never the right thing according to him.

I had to endure this situation for a whole week and when we had relief on the Saturday and walked back to the Shed his words were, 'Well mate, I don't think much of you' to which I could not help replying, 'I don't think much of you either, never once did you offer help or advice. How is one expected to learn without a single word to steer him in the right direction?'

No one in any trade can be expected to gain knowledge of it unless he is supervised and given words of encouragement by those in authority over him and I felt very disgusted that I had been subjected to this uncaring treatment.

Many years later, when I was a passed fireman, I was at Basingstoke Loco. and I saw this driver walking towards me in company with a young lad who was a picture of abject misery. Immediately my mind went back to my own situation, so I got down from the footplate to have a word with the driver asking, 'You don't remember me do you?'

He replied, saying 'No I don't', so I said, 'I remember you, you miserable old . . . . !' to the delight of the lad, obvious from the grin that lit up his downtrodden countenance.

Flare Lamp

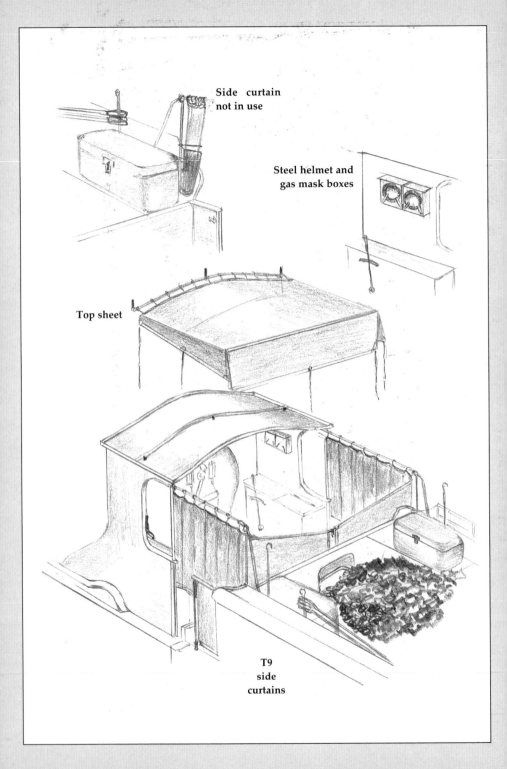

Side curtain
not in use

Steel helmet and
gas mask boxes

Top sheet

T9
side
curtains

Chapter Two

Junior Fireman - The War Years

My stay at Basingstoke came to an end quite quickly and I returned to Bournemouth on 1st April, 1940 straight back into the company of Doug, Bernard and Stan, who returned on the same day. Tom asked me if I would like the job of repairing the canvas sheets used on all locomotives to obscure the glare from the firebox so that they could not be seen from German aircraft flying overhead.

These sheets were subjected to the heat of the fire, and hot fire irons, so a good deal of time had to be spent on them to keep them in good order. I agreed to do the job. I spent many hours with a sailmaker needle and hand protector sewing patches on the filthy sheets but it was for a good purpose and so, obviously, worthwhile. However, I was not sorry when the job was taken over by a fireman who had to come off the footplate owing to ill health.

Firing turns were few and far between until the German Army made its push across France when, with the hasty withdrawal from Dunkirk, every available engine and coach was urgently required at short notice to get our troops away from the Channel Ports, where they landed. The situation changed dramatically and I was out firing most of the time.

I was soon placed in the Goods gang, being lucky enough to miss the Yard Shunter link because of the extra work that came to us at Bournemouth. The Yard Shunter link consisted of three pairs of men. The next link was the Goods gang, consisting of 14 pairs, then came the 'Old Man's' link so called because men over 60 could elect to return to this link if they did not want to progress forward to the top main line link. Next came the Push and Pull link of 12 pairs; these men were allocated their own locomotives and did all the work to Swanage, Lymington, also the 'Old Road' which was the line via Wimborne, West Moors, Ringwood between Bournemouth West and Brockenhurst, involving Push and Pull train working. Above this was No. 2 link consisting of eight pairs of men who covered Specials, sickness and holiday relief work, so their duties were very diverse, involving all kinds of work. Then finally there was No. 1 link which did all the express passenger trains to London.

My first regular driver was George Frampton, who came from my birthplace of Dorchester and he went to school with my uncles as well as knowing my parents, so straight away we had a common talking point. On our first day together we worked the 2 pm freight from Hamworthy Junction to Lyndhurst Road where we changed over with Eastleigh men and worked a passenger train to Bournemouth Central, where we had relief.

The engine for the freight was an Adams class 4-4-0 tender engine No. 666 built for express passenger work but by then relegated to local passenger and freight work.

When we started work he said, 'I don't know what you are like as a fireman, but today I want you to do the job just as I tell you; see how she steams and how easy the task can be made, but if it does not work then you do it your way and

I won't interfere'. We relieved a pair of men at Poole, then went light to Hamworthy Junction where we dropped into the small Shed making sure the fire was clean.

'Now', said George, 'start making up the fire by using hand picked lumps, not too large, and place them around the firebox making sure not to overload the fire. Then, having made a good foundation, add to the fire at regular intervals. Taking care at this stage will save yourself hard work later because it will not be necessary to use fireirons on the run to correct mistakes'.

We left on time with a light load. I exchanged hand signals with the guard, satisfying myself that the train was complete, then I picked up the single line tablet from the signalman to commence the first stage to Wimborne.

'Make sure we have the right tablet', said George, 'always read and call out the precise wording on it, then give it to the driver for him to check and confirm'.

As we started to pull up to Broadstone, the steam gauge showed we were making steam. 'Now', said George, 'put your injector on, make sure it is picking up cleanly, then cut it back as fine as you can so that you don't flood the boiler. Try to keep the water level as constant as possible by slight adjustment if necessary. Check your fire, then place coal where it is needed around the firebox, not too much at a time because it is fire that makes an engine steam, not coal, and don't keep the firehole door open too long because cold air enters it, so close it as soon as you have finished firing'.

As we approached Broadstone he shut off steam then told me to ease the door open a little to avoid blowing off steam, then to apply the tender handbrake gently to allow the train to buffer up gradually. This would prevent the guard having a rough ride when reducing our speed down to 10 mph, to give up the tablet to the signalman at Broadstone.

After I had handed it to him George said, 'Now slowly release the handbrake to allow the engine to ease away gently, so as not to snatch at the van and send the guard reeling through it'. He then gave her a small amount of regulator, gradually gathering speed then pulled the reversing lever up to 25 per cent, adding a touch more when the train was fully underway. This procedure was repeated as we dropped down into Wimborne and on George's instruction I closed down the damper to one notch, so as to control the steam pressure and partially opened the firehole door as well.

After carrying out shunting operations and just before it was time to leave George told me to lift up the damper and ease the firehole door together in readiness for the next section to Ringwood. Again the same drill was employed, then as we approached the platform we stopped at the water column to fill our tender to ensure we had enough water to complete the journey to Eastleigh Yard.

We shunted Ringwood yard making up our train to a full load of 55 wagons in length and during the shunting at convenient moments I had, on George's instruction, added to the fire and kept the water well up in the boiler.

When it was starting time we were in complete readiness for the long pull out of Ringwood and on receiving the guard's 'right away', I exchanged hand signals with him when I was sure the whole of the train was on the move.

George checked that the signal at Crow Crossing was off, saw that we were again making steam then instructed me to put on the injector, cutting it as fine as possible. The steam gauge seemed glued to the red line and a wisp of steam issued from the safety valves as I fired up, making sure, under his watchful eye, that the fire retained its shape and intensity.

The injector was still on as we passed Beaulieu Road station and at this point he told me to shut off the injector and open the door. He explained that this was to allow the water level to fall so that when we arrived at Lyndhurst Road there would be boiler space to keep the engine under control and avoid 'blowing off'.

After arrival we shunted back into the long siding, then picked up some wagon loads of pit props from the Forestry Commission's siding and put them on our train, also placing some empties in position for loading the next day. Finally, we took the engine forward towards the station so as to be able to change over with the down slow passenger train.

We changed over quickly with Eastleigh men, then, still under George's expert tuition, I was just as successful on this final lap of our journey. On arrival at our destination George said, 'Tomorrow it's up to you to do as you wish, but if today has been of help let it be your guide'.

Having seen that this was the way it should be done, how could I possibly alter it. I could but attempt to repeat the performance which I managed to do, much to my delight, for the rest of the week.

In the ensuing months George helped me in every way to become a fireman capable of doing any task efficiently and I followed his advice closely, as I had nothing but respect for him. We got on well together and helped each other in many ways, both on and off duty, lending each other tools, also assisting each other with jobs like concrete mixing, bricklaying and woodwork.

I was still his fireman when the saddest day of my life occurred. I learned that my father had been killed in action at sea. He was a Royal Marine with 22 years service to his credit, serving as a gunner on a merchant ship, the *Darlington Court* which was sunk in the Atlantic.

Soon after his death I was moved up into the 'Old Man's' link but the driver I should have been with was off sick and never did return to work but, sadly, succumbed to his illness. His place was filled by a passed fireman, Reg Sprague, who was one of those rare characters who could always hold the attention of others when conversing, being full of wit, intelligence and humour, whilst having a good knowledge of gardening as well as life in general. He hailed from Devon and never did lose the broad Devonshire dialect with which he could hold a cabin full of men transfixed.

When I think of him, my mind always goes back to the day when we had to work on an ex-London, Brighton and South Coast 2-6-0, No. 2343, and the problems that we were faced with. Earlier during that day a pair of Bournemouth men had relieved a freight from Eastleigh to work it through to Hamworthy Junction and were faced with a class of locomotive that they had not even seen before, being quite different from the engines they normally worked on. This engine was equipped with an air brake, Westinghouse air pump and a Weir water pump and on changing over the driver and fireman were given a brief rundown on these features by the Eastleigh crew, then they set off through Meyrick Park towards Poole.

The boiler started to lose steam pressure, so on went the blower and down came the pricker with the fireman frantically trying to bring her round. Although losing steam pressure, the water stayed high in the glass and when the driver shut off steam at Branksome for the descent of Parkstone Bank, the water level seemed to increase. While all this had been going on the Westinghouse air pump had been steadily pumping away, or so thought the driver, but, in fact, it had been the Wier water pump continually putting water into the boiler. As soon as the driver started to use the air brake, the Westinghouse pump started up and only then did they realize the cause of their problems with the water, now too high for comfort.

When they arrived back at Bournemouth Loco., Reg and I relieved them and they gave us a good drilling on these 'unusual' pieces of equipment then left us to clean the fire, oil the locomotive and take coal and water.

We left running light tender first to Hamworthy Junction for the 11.13 pm freight to Eastleigh Yard. When passing Parkstone station Reg touched the brake to reduce speed but we stopped very abruptly with both of us finishing up in the low fronted tender, shaken but unhurt. We looked at each other then burst out laughing, but Reg made sure that it did not happen again and we arrived at Hamworthy Junction without further incident. We had to make up our train so we started shunting as soon as we crossed the road into the Up Yard, with Reg having to repeatedly wind the lever backwards and forwards. Then he noticed an air valve placed there to assist in pulling the lever back. The seat on the driver's side was fitted directly on to the reversing lever and Reg made the mistake of opening the air valve while he was sitting on it, then, giving a hefty heave, the lever reversed sending Reg across the footplate almost into my lap, much to my amusement, also his when he got over the shock.

The rest of the shunting was finished off without problems and we left on time with a good load, stopping at Poole, where the load was increased so that it was necessary to have a banker.

The banker came out on to the back of the train but did not couple on as loose banking was permitted during steam days. He gave a couple of 'crows' on the whistle to let us know that he was ready for the off. Reg answered with two 'crows' having made certain that the starting signal was off, then opened the regulator and we were away and turned the top of the bank where the banker left us without any problems. When Reg shut off the steam for Christchurch, I gave the tender brake a few turns to bring the train comfortably together in case the distant was on, but we had the road so I slowly released it again letting the train run out so that Reg could open the regulator for the pull up to Hinton Admiral. When we had passed through Sway, Reg shut off steam so I went over to start applying the tender brake again but he stopped me saying, 'Don't bother with that Stan, I will use the air brake'. His first application was gentle but the second was far more than he had intended, almost stopping us dead. When the train slammed into us his first thought was for the guard and when we stopped at Brockenhurst he went back to make sure he was all right.

Fortunately, he was unhurt, having braced himself when he heard the train buffering up noisily, but Reg apologised for his error, explaining that he was not used to this class of locomotive. The guard gave Reg the thumbs up sign saying, 'That's alright Reg, no harm done!'.

On Saturday we were booked to work the 2 pm freight from Hamworthy Junction to Eastleigh via the 'Old Road' and as we only had the brake van we left an hour early for Wimborne. As we pulled away from the yard the air raid siren sounded and we were horrified to see a German bomber diving low over the centre of Poole, dropping bombs as it did so in the area of the town and harbour.

Reg said, 'Keep an eye on him and if he comes in our direction we will stop and take cover in that drainage ditch at the side of the line'. No sooner had he uttered these words than we were rocked by loud explosions from the opposite direction, so the brake was immediately applied and Reg and I, followed closely by the guard, beat a hasty retreat into the ditch, only to discover that the 'explosions' instead of being bombs were, in fact, gunfire from anti-aircraft guns situated on a low hill above and to the left of us. Redfaced, but none the less relieved, we climbed out of the ditch and continued on our journey. We were very amused about it later, but it was an incident we preferred to keep to ourselves.

Reg knew that I liked doing woodwork and one day he asked me if I had any suitable wood to make some tops for his front gate posts, so I made him a pair out of well seasoned oak. They still remain on those gate posts to this day, after more than 45 years but, sadly, Reg is no longer with us, having passed away quite recently.

My period of firing to Reg did not last very long, but fond memories of it still remain because this was, in terms of comradeship, the Golden Age of Railways with the war binding us all so closely together in times of both adversity and triumph.

Reg had to drop back to the Shed Turner's link when my next mate Walt Churchill decided that he did not want to progress forward, having reached 60, preferring the quieter, less hectic life in the 'Old Man's' link.

Walt was a man full of technical knowledge of steam locomotives which he taught me at every opportunity until I could answer any question that he chose to put to me. I have never forgotten his words of wisdom and on many occasions I have made use of his teachings to help others when they had to go in for their driving examination. He was a delight to work with, always cheerful, although he suffered badly with rheumatism, but he never let it interfere with his work.

We had several turns that involved tender-first running, one of them included two trips between Christchurch and Wareham usually with a '700' class 0-6-0 tender engine, which was very unpleasant during the winter months, even though we were afforded some protection by using the blackout sheets.

Visibility was very restricted and I recall one occasion when Walt stopped a bit short when running into Poole during darkness, which brought a sarcastic remark from a passenger. Walt invited him up on the footplate and much to our surprise he accepted, so we set off towards Wareham, calling at Hamworthy Junction, then Holton Heath, by which time he was shivering with the cold, also very apologetic saying, 'It beats me how you stick this, I have not seen a thing since we left Poole and how the hell you manage to find stations I'll never know. One thing is certain, it is the last time you will hear a complaint from me'.

From that day onwards he always gave us a wave and a cheery grin, also he would often produce a bag of toffees tossing half a dozen on to my seat which was on the platform side. Just goes to show that you can make friends out of the most unlikely situations.

Walt's great love was growing prize chrysanthemums which he did with a remarkable degree of success, so one day I asked him what he fed them on, to which he replied, 'Eldridge Pope's bitter after I have done with it', and judging by the blooms he brought in for anyone who requested them it was an unqualified success.

Much of the work in the 'Old Man's' Link was local passenger workmen's trains running between Christchurch and Wareham or Swanage, a little push and pull work and some short freight turns. There was a small amount of shunting, but in general the work was light without an excess of preparing or disposal duties and provided an ideal step up for firemen without having to work very early turns or night work.

We had a turn to Salisbury which was a pleasant run via West Moors with a 'T9' 4-4-0 tender locomotive at the head of a short passenger, and it provided more experience for the fireman with quite brisk running although it stopped at all stations.

The 'T9' was a free steaming locomotive with large 6 ft 7 in. driving wheels with a good turn of speed, although in adverse weather conditions they were prone to slip so care had to be taken to minimise this. However, this did not present any problem to Walt because he had the patience and skill to coax these engines away from a station no matter what the rail conditions were.

With the War gaining momentum, there was an increase in work that came our way and, as a result, promotion was rapid, so my term in the 'Old Man's' Link soon came to an end. It was much to my regret that I had to leave Walt but I am happy to say that we remained firm friends until he retired from the Railway and whenever we met there was always a smile and a cheery word, also a question to make sure I had not forgotten what he had taught me.

My next move took me into the Push and Pull Link which did nearly all of the passenger work on the Swanage branch, also the 'Old Road'. That was the line from Poole, via Broadstone, Wimborne, West Moors, Ashley Heath, Ringwood and Holmsley, joining the main line at Lymington Junction, but these trains terminated at Brockenhurst. We also had one turn down to Lymington Town during the morning as part of an 'Old Road' turn, with a quick run down and back with only a short stay, just long enough for the driver to change ends then 'Right Away' again.

In this link we had our own engines, each one being allocated to two pairs of men who were on opposite shifts, early and late. Having one's own engine gave men a sense of pride and a lot of time was spent by most men in making sure its footplate was kept clean. Also tubes were run when time permitted to make sure that the engine was steaming freely, thus making work a lot easier. Headlamps, disc boards, tools and fireirons received constant attention, again to make sure that a busy job was not a bind but a pleasure as, indeed, it was.

My mate now was Fred Smith, a very religious man, well versed in the teachings of the Bible, with a remarkable command of the English language. He was, in fact, a Lay Preacher at the local Christadelphian Church.

Our locomotive was an 'M7' tank No. 47 which I found to be easy to make steam, fairly light on the fire and a free runner but, for some unexplained reason, my opposite fireman had some difficulty and it proved to be a source of problems to him; why, I will never know. Perhaps he had not had the advantage of being taught the finer arts of firing by a man like George Frampton.

Most of the 'M7' tanks were fitted for push and pull working which was an arrangement that ruled out the necessity for an engine to run-round its train at the end of its journey. The locomotives were fitted with a Westinghouse pump which provided air enabling the driver to drive from the leading coach of the train, giving him control over the regulator, and the means to ascertain its position with an electrically operated gauge powered by batteries. The latter also provided the power to operate a bell for communication with the fireman.

When starting away with a train, the driver would give one ring on the bell, which was acknowledged by the fireman, again with one ring. The driver opened the regulator then, when under way, the fireman would place the valve gear in the desired position by means of the steam operated reversing lever. When ready to shut off steam the driver would ring the bell then close the regulator; the fireman would reply to the bell and place the reverser into full gear. The braking of the train was, of course, under the full control of the driver, but in an emergency the fireman could apply the brake and close the regulator.

We had one turn on the early shift which started off with a passenger train to Eastleigh, where we were relieved. Then for the return part of the duty we worked the 9.03 am freight from Eastleigh Yard to Bournemouth Central Goods Yard. The locomotive for this freight was nearly always the same one, No. 612 an 0-4-2 tender locomotive of the 'A12' class built by Adams in 1887. It was very small and never intended for this type of work but she would handle a full load remarkably well, providing the driver made full use of the down gradients before ascending both Sway and Pokesdown banks.

As soon as Fred saw that the distant signal was off, over would go the regulator to full to gather as much momentum as possible to make sure that the steep banks were climbed with comparative ease.

A good head of steam was of utmost importance with this type of engine but I am happy to say that this never presented me with any difficulties. The old method of 'little and often' firing and a finely cut injector was the answer and it never failed.

Fred was very annoyed on one occasion when, running into Swanage, having handed the tablet to the signalman, he failed to stop precisely at a pile of mailbags that had been placed on the platform ready for loading.

The station master approached him saying 'You knew that the mail had to be loaded, so why did you not stop so that it could be placed straight into the van, instead of having to be moved again?' Fred replied, rather testily, 'In future I will be sure to do just that, but please instruct your signalman to come and collect the tablet because I cannot give it to him and be sure of stopping on a sixpence!'

From that day forward Fred would never give up the tablet and took delight in a battle of words with the station master whenever the opportunity presented itself. This station master moved on to Brockenhurst then Bournemouth and, much to my amusement, there was many a verbal battle with Fred always coming out on top.

We were at Brockenhurst one morning waiting for the arrival of the down London train, there being a booked connection and the first loudspeaker system had just been completed a few minutes earlier. We were stopped right alongside the inspector's office when the same station master started to make the first announcement, at which Fred came over to my side of the 'M7' locomotive and opened the steam cock for the Westinghouse pump, so that it started to pound away, completely drowning out the sound coming from the system. The station master burst out of the office and angrily shouted, 'Driver, is that noise necessary, you are spoiling the effect of the loudspeakers'. Fred immediately retorted, 'It is not only necessary, it is absolutely essential, we can't move without it!' The station master turned on his heels and re-entered the office, slamming the door behind him to hide his obvious displeasure.

Fred did not enjoy the best of health, so when it was his turn for promotion he decided not to progress forward to No. 2 Link but to go into the 'Old Man's' Link, an option open to any man over sixty.

Much to my joy I was again teamed up with George Frampton and spent several months furthering my education in the art of firing. Then, under his instruction, I often did the driving, first on shunting duties, then on freight turns and finally on all types of passenger trains. He would take over the firing and I marvelled at the apparent ease with which he made any class of engine steam, yet was always able to keep complete control over the boiler, with smoke down to the minimum, without letting the locomotive 'blow off' which, of course, was a waste of coal and water. In his words he summed it up: 'Steam coming out of the safety valves does not even turn a wheel!'

It is in the company of such men that footplate work, although hard and often dirty, became to me a pleasure, or should I say privilege, that will remain forever in my thoughts, making the job one which I would not have exchanged for any other. It was with a willing heart that I went to work, even with the awful hours that we had to endure: early mornings, late nights and, often during the war, long hours on duty, missed meals, lack of sleep with little opportunity to go out to enjoy oneself.

We were at the last stage of a Swanage turn one evening 'pushing' an empty train from Wareham to Bournemouth Central on a very wild and windy night, approaching the outer home signal for Poole, which was always a very difficult signal to see. George was at the car end, which, during darkness had very poor visibility bacause the windows had to be blacked out, leaving only a small panel for the driver to see out of. I always made it a practice to look out as we approached this signal in case the driver failed to locate it. I was doing just this when a rather disturbing, although amusing, incident occurred. With the wind blowing hard against the side blackout sheet over this very exposed section of the line, it was necessary for me to push hard against it to be able to see the signal through the resulting opening, when suddenly the sheet string came undone. Then, being unable to hold it, I was forced back down on to the driver's side seat. The wind flung the sheet around me with the loose string wrapping itself firmly around the brake handle pulling it down to the full application position, bringing the train to an abrupt halt. Being completely encircled by the sheet, I could not reach the string until I managed to free myself from it and then unravelling the tangle around the brake handle, I gave George one ring on the bell and we were off again.

On arrival at Bournemouth I explained the situation to George but he pretended not to believe me saying, 'That's a likely story, you let her get low on steam so that the brake went on', grinning all over his face.

My next promotion took me into No. 2 Link, which consisted mostly of spare turns, London trips to Waterloo and also trips to Victoria on 'Airways' trains which ran from Poole to Victoria non stop. These were introduced to connect with BOAC's flying boat service to the Capital and conveyed Military and Government VIPs of the allies. When Hurn Airport was opened these trains started from Bournemouth West, stopping at Christchurch to pick up passengers, then ran non stop to Victoria station, leaving the up main at Wimbledon and running via Streatham Jn, Balham and Clapham Junction, over the main line, then down into Victoria. The motive power for these trains was nearly always a 'T9' locomotive but sometimes a SECR 4-4-0 locomotive was used. The train consisted of four Pullman coaches plus two ordinary coaches and the timing was sharp, so speeds in excess of 80 mph were necessary to time these 'Specials' which ran on an 'if required' basis.

My driver was now Bill Watts, a man of diminutive stature, but with an arm of tremendous strength which he used effectively to open the regulator wide at every opportunity that presented itself. He had a most agreeable disposition, often breaking into a grin in the most arduous situations, and always ready to enjoy a joke even if it was at his own expense. My luck certainly held when it came to mates and I was lucky enough never to have to endure the few 'miseries' that every depot seems to have its share of.

Another SE&CR class I worked on was the '01' class 0-6-0 tender engine and this was on the 'Airways' train also. We worked the up train from Bournemouth West with a 'T9' and walked back to the rear of the train to await the arrival of the engine for the down trip.

When we saw the '01' setting back towards the train we thought it was just making a shunt movement but, no, it was coupled to the train. It looked as though it had never been cleaned in its life and the small tender with its springs on the outside carried above the framings made it look only one step ahead of the *Rocket*.

My driver, Bill Watts, said to the Stewarts Lane driver, 'Where the hell did you dig this one up from?' To which he replied, 'This was the only loco. available according to the running foreman, but if you are not happy about it give him a ring!'

Bill rang the foreman who said, 'I am sorry driver, I have no other loco. available but as you are only working an empty train back you will be able to take your time'.

Bill nearly exploded at this remark replying, 'We have a train loaded with high ranking Army officers and I don't think that they would appreciate us trundling along at 30 mph on your word that we have an empty train. We will, however, do our best but any 'lost time' ticket we receive will be sent up for you to answer!'

The guard, a Bournemouth man, came up and gave us the load which consisted of four Pullman cars and two first class coaches but on seeing the '01' asked rather tentatively, 'Do you think we will make it?' Bill replied, 'Of course we will make it but we may have to stop at Southampton for water as the tender only holds 3,300 gallons and timing the train is, no doubt, going to be a bit of a problem!'

As soon as we got the guard's 'right away' signal, Bill opened up the regulator almost fully and the '01' responded by moving away quite briskly from Victoria's No. 17 platform. We had a full tender of good quality Yorkshire hard coal and I fired steadily with it and was delighted that the engine responded so well to my efforts, moving over to the blowing off point and staying there when I put the injector on and cut it down as finely as I could.

Taking the train easily over the restricted speed area through Streatham, Balham and Tooting, we crossed over to the main through line at Wimbledon and were a little up on time at Hampton Court Junction. Bill was working the engine a little heavier then he would have a 'T9' but I had no difficulty in keeping up the steam pressure and the water was just bobbing under the top nut. But with the increase in speed the locomotive was bouncing about like a pea on a drum. The pull up from Woking to Pirbright Junction took some speed out of us but Bill left the controls as they were, then as we approached Farnborough he eased the regulator slightly as we regained momentum.

To try to match the speed of a 'T9' would have been foolish but I guessed we were running at about 65 mph which was probably faster than the '01' had been driven for some time, being used almost exclusively on freight or shunting work.

We passed Worting Junction only two minutes down, but I had kept the boiler pressure and the water level at a very healthy state so this had been a big factor in our good progress. As we turned the top of the incline at Litchfield my thoughts turned to an amusing incident at this point when I was working with driver Fred Tollerfield. On an up fast train Fred took off his cap and held it to his chest reverently lowering his head while I looked at him mystified. When I questioned his action he pointed to the gradient board at the side of the track with both of its arms pointing downwards explaining, 'That is the Saviour's Cross, and at that point if you are not doing too well in either direction you can shut off steam and coast'. I just could not help laughing and on countless occasions afterwards I thought of his words, but only twice was it necessary to test the wisdom of them, once as a fireman and once as a driver. This, however, was not one of them!

In those days, few locomotives were fitted with speedometers and as we gathered speed on the downgrade run to Southampton, we must have passed the 70 mark but the coal was being shaken forward and spilled out all over the footplate. Bill was determined not to lose too much time but in the end, with dust flying everywhere, he shut off steam and let her coast. I tried the water tap fitted on the tender front at Eastleigh and the water was only just trickling out, so Bill decided we had better take some at Southampton.

We stopped at the water column and the station inspector came rushing up saying, 'You are not booked to stop here Driver!' Bill's reply was, 'I thought it better to stop here for water than take the risk of running out of it somewhere in the New Forest'. The inspector had just realized what locomotive we had and his reaction was exactly the same as Bill's had been at Victoria.

As soon as we had taken sufficient water we were on our way again, with Bill taking the '01' smartly away from Southampton while I fired her up again and was pleased to see her respond at once. We went round the curve at Redbridge well up to the speed limit, then Bill dropped the lever over one nick and gave her full regulator to gain speed for the rise up to Beaulieu Road, keeping her like that until we sighted the distant signal for Brockenhurst. As he closed the regulator to coast through the station the '01' blew off steam, so close was the needle to the red line.

As soon as we cleared the platform Bill was into it again keeping the speed up to climb the bank towards Sway, and keeping her going after we turned the top, bringing her up to 65 mph at New Milton and in excess of 70 mph as we ran down Hinton Bank. Closing the regulator as we sighted the distant signal, Bill brought her to a perfect stop at Christchurch. Glancing at his watch, he said, 'Not bad, we are only eight minutes late and that includes taking water at Southampton Central. I thought we would lose a week!'

On receiving the guard's signal to start, Bill opened the regulator gently at first, then after pulling the lever up to 40 per cent gave her the lot, storming up Pokesdown Bank with sparks flying from the chimney, but failing to dislodge the steam pressure needle from the line it had seemingly been glued to all the way down.

We had relief at Bournemouth Central on the through road after an excellent trip, despite the rough ride and the dust that just could not be controlled, but although we were tired and very dusty, we were well satisfied with our performance. I went home with a deep feeling of achievement, happy in the knowledge that I had not let Bill down and that we had done our very best, so no one could ask for more from us.

Bill never did receive a 'lost time' ticket; the guard would not issue one!

I well remember one occasion when working with Bill during a week where the first part of the duty was to work a passenger train from Brockenhurst to Eastleigh where we had relief, then to walk down to the Shed, prepare a locomotive and work a parcel train from Eastleigh to Bournemouth. The normal motive power was an Adams 4-4-0 type engine, but one night, much to our surprise, we were given a 'T9' No. 281 for no apparent reason. But when we arrived in the siding at Eastleigh we were informed that our parcels train had been cancelled and we had to work some empty coaches to Bournemouth West instead. On attaching to our train we were greeted with the news that we had a total of 17 coaches which was far in excess of a full load, so Bill phoned Control only to be told that it was imperative that this train ran. Time was unimportant, no larger engine was available and no assistance was to be had to which Bill replied, 'Alright, we will take them on condition that we get a run through both Brockenhurst and Christchurch so that we can approach both banks at speed to give us a reasonable chance of climbing them'.

We set off from Eastleigh at a leisurely pace and I gradually built up a good fire, making sure to keep the steam pressure over on the line, thus giving Bill all the power possible when he needed it. As soon as we saw that the distant signal for Brockenhurst was 'off', Bill's muscular right arm came into play and over went the regulator to full, with the lever (cut-off) down on 40 per cent, thus making the top of the bank without difficulty, where Bill pulled the lever up to 25 per cent, easing the regulator down to half, then drifting along until we sighted the distant for Christchurch.

With a 'clear' indication in view, the regulator was again fully opened but the lever was not altered because the long down grade gave us time to gain speed, but as we had no speedometer I could only guess that we were well up to the permitted limit of 60 mph.

It was necessary to increase the valve travel as we neared Pokesdown as our speed was down to less than 30 mph, but, again, no real difficulty was experienced and Bill shut off steam at Boscombe to coast through Bournemouth Central at 15 mph. With such a long train it was not possible to make a normal approach to No.4 platform which was the longest at Bournemouth West, so the signalman had set the road towards the goods yard then out again across the points into the station which, when cleared, brought a call from Bill, 'Give her some sand Stan!' I pulled open the front sand lever which was on my side of the cab, closing it again as we came to a halt close to the buffer stops, having sanded the rail for the full length of No. 4 platform. On receiving the tip from the shunter, we pushed our train up the fairly sharp incline to the carriage berthing siding without so much as a slip, to our relief and amazement. The next day the coaches were used to convey American troops down to Weymouth for embarkation on the ships in readiness for the D-Day landings, so our efforts did contribute a little towards the success of that operation.

The very next night we had to work a Special from Ringwood and set off from Bournemouth Shed with engine No. 695 an 0-6-0 built about 1897 by Dübs, running light via Poole and Wimborne with destination as yet unknown. On arrival we were met by the shunter who let us into the Up Yard via the ground frame points, where a scene of feverish activity was perceived. Coloured Americans of the United States Army Air Corps were loading objects into open wooden freight wagons, the floors of which were covered in straw, totalling 21 wagons in all. The wagon next to the locomotive and the one next to the guard's van were not being loaded, but were still lined with straw. The guard gave us the load and instructions to be observed whilst working the train, which was for Wylye, between Salisbury and Westbury, telling us that the speed throughout was 15 mph, except over crossover roads when the speed was 5 mph.

A burly Top Sergeant with an armful of stripes climbed up on to the footplate and in a southern drawl said, 'Don't shake the goddam things about, they are all set to go off!' Bill asked him what we were carrying and he said 'Anti personnel fragmentation bombs fitted with fuses and rods to make them burst above ground, so take it nice and easy!'

When we received the 'Right away' signal from the guard, Bill eased open the regulator and kept strictly to the speed limit making sure that we did not emit any sparks from the chimney, which this class of locomotive was very prone to do. Our route was via Brockenhurst, Eastleigh, Romsey and Salisbury, a journey which took half the night, during which time we had two air raid warnings but, thankfully, no signs of enemy aerial activity. On arrival at Wylye, the wagons were being unloaded even before I had time to uncouple, again by USAAF troops. Later that day we learned that our own soldiers, along with the Americans, had started landing in Normandy and the bombs we had carried were being dropped even before we had signed off duty, so again we had done our bit for the War effort.

I was not with Bill Watts for long as we had an influx of drivers from other depots around this period and this meant that passed firemen who were doing 100 per cent driving turns were put back firing, so I had to drop down into the Push and Pull Link again. However, my luck still held and my mate was now Bill Smith, our own locomotive being 'M7' tank No. 106, a good strong, free steaming beauty that we kept in immaculate condition.

Bill Smith was a jovial man, with a love of stamp collecting and gardening. In fact he was something of an expert on Philately, knowing exactly what to buy in quantity in order to make money at a future date to further increase his collection. We soon established a friendship that was only terminated by his early death before he reached retirement age and a working relationship in which we had complete trust in each other, making our daily routine very enjoyable as, indeed, it should be.

On one of our turns we were booked to work the 4.32 pm from Bournemouth West to Brockenhurst via the 'Old Road' and at times we had to attach the 'Airways' train, simply to work it back in stages to Victoria when it was not required for an up Special.

The normal train was two coaches which we pushed to Brockenhurst but with an additional six coaches it was the accepted practice to pull the train which meant shunting the 2-set, then running bunker first, a dusty uncomfortable trip being assured.

On the first occasion we were required to work this formation, Bill said, 'Well what about it, do we pull or push, its up to you!' So knowing full well the extra work involved, I said 'Let's push', to which he readily agreed.

He made his way up to the driving car end, happy in the knowledge that he could rely on me to keep No. 106 steaming, to use the large ejector in the event of over braking if necessary and to make sure we had sufficient water on leaving Ringwood. No. 106 was very economical on water and, although it was necessary to work her harder with the additional 250 tons, we always managed to complete our journey of 32 miles without the need to fill the water tank at Ringwood, a fact that some drivers found difficult to believe. On arrival at Brockenhurst, we just had to shunt the Airways train back into the up siding and were then ready for the return journey back to Bournemouth West. I always liked to be right on time on this turn because it meant I could go out for the evening and it was important to have a break on a week of late turns.

We had some interesting work in addition to our push and pull duties, especially on Sundays when we worked longer distance trains to Basingstoke or Waterloo.

This work served as a useful breaking-in period for firemen to work on larger locomotives but my time in No. 2 Link had given me lots of experience on 'Schools', 'Arthurs', 'Nelsons' and also 'Remembrance' class engines. 'Remembrance' class locomotives were used on fast passenger trains but they were never really up to the work, especially when trains were often 13 or 14 coaches long. They were difficult to fire to as it was necessary to crack the coal up small and feed it through a firehole door that was fitted with a small slot not much bigger than a letter flap. By using this small door these locomotives could be made to steam freely but it required skill and concentration with no margin for error and some firemen found it easier to use the larger door. However, with a heavy fast train this had an adverse effect on the engine's steaming and with even a small drop in the boiler pressure, especially uphill, it soon affected the driver's ability to keep the train on time. In consequence these engines were not popular.

The 'Schools' class locomotives were our main line engines being allocated to the top link men and they were a delightful locomotive to work on. Although they were only 4-4-0s they were fast and free steaming but, during the War years, they were often overloaded. At the time they were my favourite locomotive and I found them easy to fire to, fairly light on coal, which was readily accessible as the tender had a built up front so that coal could be stacked well up at the forward part of the tender.

The worst feature was the small water capacity making it necessary to fill the tender more often than 'Nelsons' or 'Arthurs'. Locomotives Nos. 924-933 were assigned to Bournemouth but with heavier trains coming into service it became necessary to replace the 'Schools' and they were superseded by the 'Lord Nelson' class locomotives, several being allocated to Bournemouth Depot.

The 'Schools' class were often expected to haul 14 coaches during the war, with frequent stops and their only failing was the fact that they were inclined to slip which, of course, was due to the 4-4-0 wheel arrangement. The only time I had a bad trip on one was when, during the war, we were using seaborne coal which, after being loaded on and off ships, was nothing more than dust. The driver I was with was a moody individual who was not happy because he could not get a 'pint' before coming to work and, as a result, was in a contrary mood.

We relieved the crew on No. 928 *Stowe* and steam pressure was well back with the water level down to half a glass. The fire looked just like a heap of soot and the coal in the tender like gunpowder, so it was obvious to me that the fire needed lifting up with the dart to get some life into it. I took the chain off the fireirons and lifted the dart up, but Tom, the driver, stopped me with a curt, 'You can leave that alone, I'll tell you when to use a fireiron!' so I reluctantly chained them up again. The other crew had filled the tender up for us and in the five minutes we had stood there the steam pressure had risen to 180 lb. and the water was at the mark.

Tom pulled away when he received the guard's tip and with the pull of the exhaust I could see coal was needed at the front of the firebox, but the problem was, just how do you fill holes with gunpowder against such opposition. All I could do was feed the light parts of the fire by distributing the coal around the box with a flick of the wrist and in so doing achieved a similar effect to an oil burner, but the fire was dead and lifeless under the door and needed to be loosened. So I made a second move to free the fireirons but was again stopped by the driver. We did manage to arrive at Southampton without any loss of time.

After topping up the tender with water I tried to find some lumps in the coal but none of it was as big as a pea! I knew we were sure to be in trouble before we made the top of the bank at Litchfield tunnel. Sure enough, before we reached Wallers Ash loop it was all too obvious that we would never make it, so Tom blew up the recognised whistle code to be let into the loop for a blow up. We stopped at the top end of the loop and without a glance at Tom I got the dart down from the tender, fully expecting to be told to replace it, but no such command came, so I lifted the fire up with it and immediately it burst into life with the steam gauge moving around rapidly.

The train that left Bournemouth 10 minutes after us sped by with its driver giving a derisory one short, one long on the whistle and a hand signal that is definitely not in the Rule Book!

By the time we again got the road, the needle was right over on the 220 lb. mark with the water just bobbing under the top nut so, off we went and I started firing systematically around the box with the dust and No. 928 stayed there. On went the injector which I cut as fine as I could. The needle stuck to the 220 lb. mark as if glued and when Tom eased her back at the top of the bank, I had to drop down the half door, which I had been using, to prevent her from blowing off. This is how she stayed until we passed Clapham Junction when I eased the damper down to reduce steam so that she would stay quiet at Waterloo.

We had relief on arrival and made our way down to the canteen for a cup of tea for which Tom insisted on paying together with a large slice of bread pudding; warm and delicious. He made no comment about the trip but whenever I worked with him after that he just let me fire in my own way and we never had another bad trip.

The 'Lord Nelson' class were much more powerful, capable of handling any train and had a larger flatter firebox making it easy to maintain the boiler pressure of 220 lb. per square inch. But a different technique had to be adopted, and I found that letting the right hand slide on the shovel kept the blade down; then the front of the firebox was reached without difficulty with the coal keeping well below the brick arch, which, if fouled, soon affected the excellent steaming qualities. They were, however, much harder to dispose of when it came to cleaning the fire, with their long fireboxes and it was an advantage to be strong and muscular which, fortunately, I was.

Some of the 'Nelsons' were fitted with 'drop' doors, thus making it easier to clean the fire but care had to be taken to make sure that the mechanism was kept clean and well oiled or it was prone to jamming. These locomotives were masters of the job and I enjoyed working on them, being quite truthfully able to say that I never had a rough trip on one, that is to say I was never short of steam at any time. The only feature I did not like was the smokebox which accumulated a lot of ash and the job of cleaning one out was hot and dirty, especially if it was windy when the ash would get in your eyes, often with painful results. There was no easy way to do this chore, it was a case of grin and bear it, which was not always possible. Fortunately, this work was mostly carried out by men in the lower links but everyone had a share during their career, no one could escape it.

It was during my partnership with Bill Smith that I married my wife, Joan, and she has proved to be everything a railwayman has need of in a job that, to say the least, is unsocial, hard and dirty. She is an excellent cook, always able to cope with the ever changing hours on duty that is the curse of railway work, producing meals in quick time to fit in with my duties. Sunday work has always meant that outings were few and far between and coping with our four children could not have been easy with me away from home at times when a man is most needed. I take my hat off to her and thank her for a very happy married life. Long may it continue!

We had a Sunday turn to Basingstoke where we had relief and made our way to the Church Army canteen to get a much needed cup of tea. As it was late evening we had to find our way in the blackout to the building where we picked our way through dozing servicemen and women to the counter.

The elderly attendant, also dozing, was brought back to life with a loud rap and on our request for tea took two mugs from a shelf, placing one under the tap of a large tea urn. An outsize enamel jug was simmering on a low gas and she emptied the hot water into the top of the urn which was full to the brim with tea leaves. She then turned on the tap waiting for the water to soak its way down through the soggy mass, which took about three minutes. It is difficult to describe the evil brew but we paid our penny a cup, gulped it down bravely, then beat a hasty retreat in case we were offered a second cup.

The War years were hard on train crews as we never knew for sure just how long we were likely to work. The longest turn of duty I ever had to work was with driver George Coomber when we set out to do a normal passenger turn on a Sunday afternoon, starting work at 2.00 pm. When we signed on duty, the running foreman asked George if he would work a Special 'Airways' train as no one else was available who knew the Road. George agreed on condition that I went with him which, of course, I was happy to do.

We arrived at Bournemouth West with a 'T9' locomotive No. 284 where we were informed that the plane had been delayed so we settled down for a long wait. After three hours, still no news was to be had so we were asked to change over with a pair of Eastleigh men and work their passenger train to Basingstoke, then to come home passenger on the 7.48 pm from Waterloo. The 7.48 pm left on time but as it was approaching Weybridge a German plane was hit by anti-aircraft fire and crashed on the line not far in front of it, completely blocking all four roads at that point. The driver stopped short of it but, of course, could not continue his journey, his train, however, was not damaged and no one was hurt.

The next train to leave London for Bournemouth was the down Mail which was diverted via Chertsey and Byfleet Junction to get it past the obstruction. Just after it left Waterloo the lines at Staines received a direct hit from a string of bombs, effectively bringing all train services to a halt.

The Basingstoke running foreman informed us of the situation and suggested we settle down for the night as there was no way of getting home. At 6.00 am he told us that a freight train had left north London destined for Poole, travelling over the Great Western lines before joining the Southern at Basingstoke. He asked us to relieve the train on arrival, which turned out to be 8.45 am, our stops being Micheldever, Eastleigh and Brockenhurst. The locomotive was No. 503 hauling a long string of wagons, loaded with a variety of merchandise, including oil for Micheldever, where we were required to set down the full ones and pick up some empties. Once inside the yard there the shunter made use of us, having got permission from Control to do so, thus the next 1½ hours was spent in making sure that there was plenty of oil in position for unloading.

It was after 11.00 am when we finally left to make the next leg of our journey to Eastleigh where, on arrival, George phoned the running foreman and asked for relief, only to be told that he did not have an available man in the Depot so we were now committed to carry on to Bournemouth. After detaching a batch of wagons for Portsmouth Naval Base, we picked up wagons filled with jerrycans of petrol for the US Army depot at West Moors which meant that they had to be detached at Brockenhurst. With a train of 90 wagons we did not leave Eastleigh until 1.15 pm, by which time we were both very tired, hungry and dirty, so we were far from amused when we were let into the goods loop at Southampton Central where we fretted for 30 minutes waiting for a pathway to Brockenhurst.

I made use of the delay by shovelling some coal forward as it was now well back in the tender, while George walked to the signal box at Millbrook to make sure that relief would be waiting for us on arrival at Bournemouth.

When we finally got the road, we were on our way to Brockenhurst where, after detaching the petrol, then picking up some wagons for Poole, we were again held for the passing of a passenger train. When we at last left we both breathed a sign of relief that this was the final leg of the trip and George opened the regulator steadily at first then as the couplings stretched out, he gave her full power to gain as much momentum as possible before we reached the steepest part of the bank in front of us. This presented us with no difficulty and we were soon over the top. George eased the regulator for the downhill run towards Christchurch, where we took the curve at the maximum permitted speed, again with the purpose of making the ascent of Pokesdown Bank as easy as possible.

We ran into Bournemouth Central at 4.00 pm, exactly 26 hours after signing on duty the previous day. We should have been on duty at 11.00 am that morning; in fact, we were listed as absent from duty as the Bournemouth running foreman had not been informed that we were still on duty.

With a 12 hour off duty clause in operation, we were, of course, unable to sign on duty for a Monday turn, so we were paid for it just the same. That was the only time I ever got paid for staying at home, but I went to bed when I arrived home after explaining to my mother what had happened as she was frantic with worry, then once in bed I slept for 19 hours.

Shortly after this episode we were working a freight train from Poole to

Eastleigh when the air raid sirens started to wail as we passed Totton signal box. We were running between Millbrook and Southampton where ships were berthed in the docks, each one having a barrage balloon above it attached by a cable to a winch mounted on the dock. Suddenly we heard machine gun fire and saw a Messerschmidt ME 109 diving towards the ships firing at each balloon in turn, setting fire to several of them. We expected the pilot to turn his guns on us but he seemed set on destroying as many balloons as possible. However, light anti-aircraft cannon fire opened up and he climbed steeply away disappearing into the nearest cloud, leaving the air full of black smoke and burning fragments.

On another occasion, we had worked a train from Bournemouth to Waterloo and then travelled by bus to Victoria to work an 'Airways' Special back to Christchurch non stop, then on to Bournemouth Central where we were booked relief. We arrived at Victoria, passing through the main concourse on our way to No. 17 platform where our train was waiting with a 'T9' class No. 337 at its head. We had just climbed on to the footplate when we saw the ticket office suddenly erupt in flames, having been hit by several incendiary bombs and I shuddered at the thought that we had passed that spot only minutes earlier. We were not sorry when we got the guard's 'Right Away' signal and we lost no time in getting away from London, never a nice place to be in Wartime.

When the Home Guard was first formed under the name Local Defence Volunteers, I joined up and was given an armband, after which I was informed that our unit would be solely concerned with the guarding of railway equipment and installations such as signal boxes, bridges as well as important rail junctions. On my first night on guard duty, in company with another young fireman, we were stationed at a tunnel in Meyrick Park. Becoming bored after two hours just standing there, we decided to patrol the track towards Bournemouth West and had just reached a road bridge when we heard a German plane overhead which was making peculiar popping sounds, giving us the impression that he had engine trouble. We turned back at the bridge and we noticed what appeared to be sparks floating upwards, so we stood fascinated by this, but at a loss for an explanation. Then my companion shouted out 'That's not sparks going up, its tracer bullets coming down!' We immediately dashed back under the bridge for cover only just making it before a hail of bullets swept through the track sending ballast flying in all directions. These, we later found out, were aimed at a searchlight situated on high ground in the Park.

Two incidents that occurred during the war may be of interest involving 'T9' No. 120 and the RAF's 257 Squadron; coincidently I was to work on No. 120 and the squadron's namesake locomotive at a much later date on the Swanage Railway. Firstly, a little known incident involving the 'T9' happened one morning on the down Brockenhurst Goods at Wool during shunting operations when the driver, with two wagons attached to the engine, pulled forward over the level crossing for a run-round movement. Stopping clear of the crossover points, they were in a position close to the Police Station when, suddenly, a lone Messerschmidt ME 109, which had been circling above, dived to the attack sweeping low with machine guns and cannon blazing. The fireman jumped from the engine to find cover but was wounded slightly as No. 120 was raked with bullets and cannon shells. By some miracle the boiler was not hit but the smokebox was holed. The outer cladding of the tender was holed many times, but the main water tank, being made of fairly heavy metal, withstood the onslaught. The cab was also hit a number of times by bullets, some coming in through the fireman's side front window severing the steam pipe to the hydrostatic cylinder lubricator and filling the cab with steam. The driver, who if my memory serves me right was 'Nobby' Clark, was looking around the side of the cab when three bullets hit the very thick edging strip just alongside his right ear. Luckily for him, the bullets failed to penetrate although splinters from it cut his neck badly.

There were two steel boxes attached to the cab on the fireman's side for the crew to place their gas masks and tin hats in, and these stopped the bullets that pierced the cab side from passing through the footplate and hitting the driver. The boxes were badly distorted but, I am glad to relate, they undoubtedly saved the driver's life.

Two cannon shells hit No. 120, but again luck played a hand. One hit the lower part of the smokebox where it is joined onto the main frames at a level that is lined with fire bricks and forms the floor on the inside. The shell exploded making a dent ¾ of an inch deep and left a pattern of lines radiating from it that closely resembled a child's drawing of the sun. The second shell hit the coupling rod at its thickest point, tearing a chunk from it but causing no real damage.

Both the driver and the fireman were taken to hospital to have their wounds treated. A relief crew were sent by taxi from Dorchester to clear the line and take the locomotive to the engine shed there. At the time of the attack there were several high ranking 'Red Tab' Officers on the platform of Wool station and there could have been a fearful slaughter if the pilot had directed his attention to them instead.

The second incident involved 257 Squadron of the RAF when, whilst stationed at Warmwell, they were the target of an early morning 'hit and run' raid by German fighter planes. A friend of mine, an engine cleaner at Basingstoke while I was on loan there, was now in the Army, having been politely asked to resign from the Southern Railway for a boyish prank that went seriously wrong. He was due for leave that day and was crossing the airfield where his unit was stationed to protect it from possible airborne attack, when planes swept over the runway spraying bullets in all directions. He dived head first into a slit trench and, as he did so, he felt a heavy blow to his foot but no pain. When the planes had passed over he looked at his foot fearing the worst, but much to his relief he realised that he was not wounded, but nevertheless was amazed to find a machine gun bullet embedded in the leather heel of his boot. On his way home to Basingstoke, he had to change trains at Bournemouth Central, so having time to spare whilst waiting for a connection, he called into the engine shed to see if I was around. He told me his story and showed me the bullet firmly lodged between the layers of his boot heel. He carried that bullet around with him for years afterwards as a Good Luck Charm.

Another incident I well remember occurred on Sunday 23rd May, at 1 pm, when Bournemouth was the target for a hit and run raid by a mixed bag of Messerschmidt ME 109s and Focke-Wulf FW 190s fighter bombers.

I was the fireman that day on the station shunter on 'M7' tank No. 112 which was the regular engine for this duty, the driver being Bill Selby who always worked this turn. The air raid siren had sounded earlier when we were standing under the station's glass canopy so Bill told the shunter, who was enjoying a cup of tea, that we would move up outside the parcels' office to be well clear of the glass roof. We had only been there a few moments when the planes coming in low over the sea to escape detection, circled above Bournemouth Central Goods Yard at minimum altitude, making for the station. They were deterred from attacking it by a hail of fire from 16 Lewis guns mounted in groups of four on top of the Post Office Sorting Office, which is in the station approach road. One FW190 dropped almost to ground level then had to pull up sharply to avoid hitting the parcel office roof. In fact it was so low that I could see the pilot clearly. When the gunfire had started Bill got down on the floor of 112 and entreated me to do the same but, being young and foolhardy, I took no notice as I did not want to miss any of the action that was going on. At this stage the fighter bombers started to release their bombs, the first of which landed on a garage in the main road doing a lot of damage and sending debris flying in all directions. A bomb splinter came down through the low canopy outside the lost property office and landed right alongside No. 112. I got down to pick it up only to find it was too hot to handle, so I dropped it with a yell, much to the amusement of Bill, now sitting on an upturned bucket but still down on the cab floor.

The main roof glass panels started to fall, whether dislodged by the explosions or hit by bullets and cannon shells I don't know but I was thankful that Bill had decided to move because in no time at all the platforms were covered in shattered glass.

Fortunately, the station inspector had had the presence of mind to make all passengers go down into the subway between the platforms in case just such an incident should occur, so no one was hurt.

My friend, Doug Scott, had a very lucky escape as he was cycling home after having been on parade in the Home Guard drill hall which was about half a mile from the station. When as he was passing the Methodist Church a bomb crashed through the roof, without exploding, shot out through the glass windows, hit the road along side him, causing a rush of air that knocked him off his bicycle, then bounced over the shops opposite to explode on hitting the ground at the back of them.

Doug's only injury was a cut elbow, plus a hole in his uniform sleeve, but this did not deter him from going back to the aid of Canadian airmen who had been in the Metropole Hotel when it received a direct hit, killing several of their number and injuring many more who were drinking in the bar, including some civilians. A Royal Marine was helping in rescue work when he was struck on the head by falling masonry and badly injured, so all those who did not have 'tin hats' including Doug, were sent home.

The raid only lasted a few minutes, but left a lot of damage to the town as our largest departmental store was gutted by fire and several more were badly hit, but far worse was the number of killed and injured, but by good fortune none of them were railwaymen.

We only had one man killed from our Depot and this was a driver, Ben Chapman, who was in bed when a land mine landed near his house doing terrible damage to a residential area and regrettably killing him outright.

Working with driver Alf Boston, we were booked to relieve a freight train from Micheldever to Hamworthy Junction at Eastleigh and it arrived with a 'WD' 2-8-0 hauling a loaded train of 90 wagons. The Eastleigh driver explained that the engine was not steaming at all well, because the tender contained only small domestic type briquettes.

As we pulled away from the station I had a careful look at the fire and it was not at all encouraging. Instead of burning up brightly it was just a dead looking pink, despite the fact that the blower was fully opened. Adding more of the briquettes to the fire produced a sulphurous smoke and they only seemed to smoulder rather than ignite, gradually turning pink then dissolving into a grey dust. A vigorous pull through with the pricker did little to bring the ailing fire back to life, but I carefully cracked up more of the briquettes, taking care not to grind them into dust with the coalpick.

We followed a local passenger train down as far as Redbridge and as we were drifting along using very little steam, I managed to fill the boiler and the 'WD' was now almost over to blowing off point. As soon as the passenger train had cleared the junction on its way to Salisbury, we were given the road and Alf opened up the regulator for the climb through Lyndhurst Road, up to Beaulieu Road station.

I fired steadily, feeding the fire with fist sized pieces of the briquettes but all that I could produce was a pink glow which rapidly turned to a dusty grey. The steam pressure fell slowly back until the brake started to go on at 100 lb. per square inch and we ground to a halt just short of the top of the gradient. It took 20 minutes to get enough steam to restart the train and turn the top, but the effort brought about a rapid fall in the boiler pressure and we arrived outside of Brockenhurst in a very depleted state. We were almost stopped at the home signal before it was raised to let us into the loop line and we just managed to get to the end of the platform, only to have the brake go on again which left the tail part of our 90 wagon long train across the main Lymington to Southampton Road, blocking all traffic to and from those towns.

We were met by the shunter who indignantly exclaimed, 'The least you could have done was to get them inside the yard!' to which Alf replied, 'This was the very most we could achieve!' I had made several attempts to open the front damper to admit more air under the fire, but could not budge it one inch so, as soon as we stopped I took the coalpick round to the front of the cab and gave the crank that led down to the damper a tap to get it open. Immediately, I was enveloped in steam and showered with hot water and ballast, so I hastily hit the crank in the opposite direction and much to my relief it subsided as quickly as it had started. What I had taken for a damper was the blow down valve, the very last thing I wanted to open.

The shunter ran to the nearest phone to get the shunting engine to come to our assistance so that we could clear the crossing and get the road traffic moving again.

As soon as we were inside the yard we were released and we went to the end of the shunting neck to clean the fire. It took me 40 minutes of non stop shovelling to remove a mountain of fine grey dust from the firebox, while Alf tried to find some decent coal with which to make the fire up but met with very little success. He did, however, manage to unearth enough for me to make a bed of real fire before it was necessary to add those awful briquettes.

The shunter came to see if we were ready to drop back on to our train which was now complete, telling us that if we were not away in 10 minutes we would have to wait an hour for a pathway as the signalman was not prepared to risk the possibility of further delay to passenger services.

With the boiler pressure building up nicely, I coupled on to our full load train, then Alf whistled up for the signal, which was pulled off almost at once, and we pulled steadily out of the yard. After exchanging hand signals with the guard to confirm that the whole of the train was on the move, I started to shovel the briquettes evenly around the firebox, but the effect was just as it had been before.The boiler pressure fell back alarmingly.

The pull out of Brockenhurst Yard is severe and by the time we had reached the top of the bank we were back to 100 lb. and I had not put the injector on for fear of reducing the pressure even more, causing the brakes to be applied.

Once over the top, Alf eased the regulator right back and I was able to put some water into the boiler which by now was becoming uncomfortably low.

As soon as we had cleared Sway station, Alf closed the regulator and we coasted down through New Milton, gathering speed as we approached Hinton Admiral. The boiler water was now at a healthy level so I shut off the injector to allow the steam pressure to rise, which it did, but at a tantalisingly slow rate, until we spotted the distant signal for Christchurch and by this time we had only 170 lb. pressure.

Alf opened the regulator slowly to tighten the couplings, then fully to gain momentum for the steep climb up through Pokesdown, rounding the curve at Christchurch at 60 mph, whilst I tried to liven up the fire by pulling the pricker through it, only to see most of it disappear in a flurry of dust. Back to the shovel I went swinging it with an easy rhythm, distributing the briquettes evenly, desperately trying to maintain steam but to no avail. However, we just managed to crawl through Boscombe station where Alf closed the regulator to coast into Bournemouth.

Our relief was waiting for us and I felt rather ashamed at having to hand over the 'WD' in such a depleted state. My relief was a senior fireman and he said, 'Don't worry, I'll soon put her right'. The next day he told me that they had to stop for a blow up after only 2 miles, then on arrival at Hamworthy had to clean the fire and rake out the ashpan in the small depot that was there. He said the ashpan was filled to capacity and only had one damper, so could only be raked out from one end and the wind was blowing through the shed so that when he emerged from under the engine he closely resembled a ghost, being covered from head to toe in pale grey dust. To be sure of getting back light to Bournemouth depot without further problem, he made the fire up with good Welsh coal from the coal stack; after that, performance was superb!

Schools' class 4-4-0 No. 925 *Cheltenham* is seen at speed at Hersham in 1938 on a down Bournemouth/Swanage train. This view shows clearly the condition these engines were kept in by Bournemouth engine cleaners.   *LPC*

An up Bournemouth train headed by a 'King Arthur' class 4-6-0 passes through Beaulieu Road station *c.* 1938.   *R. Smith Collection*

'Merchant Navy' class 4-6-2 No. 35026 *Lamport & Holt Line* passes through Pirbright with an up Bournemouth train soon after its construction in December 1948. The engine is carrying the early blue British Railways livery which was used for passenger engines at this time.

Author's Collection

My old mate Syd Futcher is seen on the up platform at Bournemouth Central on his last day before his retirement in April 1950. Syd is shaking hands with his son in this view, whilst looking on from the footplate of 'West Country' class 4-6-2 *Saunton* are driver Syd Friend and myself.

Author's Collection

An unidentified Southern 'mogul' with an up Bournemouth local train crosses the Battledown Flyover. The flyover carries Southampton-Waterloo trains over the Salisbury-Exeter line, 10th May, 1952. *E.R. Morten*

'S15' class 4-6-0 No. 30507 heads a down freight for Eastleigh at Worting Junction as it tackles the gentle upgrade towards Litchfield, 10th May, 1952. On the left can be seen the embankment which leads from Battledown Flyover. *E.R. Morten*

Canadian National Railway's 1000 hp Alco 'Switcher' No. 8457 was the first Canadian locomotive I worked on. This view was taken during a tea break, during my stay in 1952.
Author

CNR '41XX' class 2-10-2 No. 4019 'helper' locomotive assists a 2-unit Fairbanks-Morse diesel electric locomotive with a load in excess of 4,800 tons, at Toronto in July 1952. *Author*

'L' class 4-4-0 No. 31777 is seen at Fareham station on a Portsmouth-Bournemouth West train in August 1952. These engines were sometimes used on the Bournemouth-Victoria 'Airways' trains during World War II. *Real Photographs*

'H15' class 4-6-0 No. 30480 is seen near Brookwood with an up local train from Basingstoke, 20th July, 1953. *E.R. Morten*

My own engine 'West Country' class No. 34093 *Saunton* arrives at Waterloo on an up Bournemouth train in August 1965. She is seen here in rebuilt form, but I much preferred her as designed by O.V.S. Bulleid, in her original condition. *Real Photographs*

BR Standard class '4MT' 2-6-0 No. 76027 approaches Winchester City station with a down train, 10th September, 1955. These engines were widely used on local passenger and freight work. They were a joy to work on, with the exception of when they were used for shunting. *E.R. Morten*

'West Country' class 4-6-2 No. 34095 *Brentnor* approaches St Denys with the 'Bournemouth Belle' on 20th March, 1966. Due to engineering work the train had been diverted via the Netley line.
Roy Panting

A down freight leaves Eastleigh behind 'King Arthur' class 4-6-0 No. 30783 *Sir Gillemere* for Southampton Docks, 1st August, 1957. A Hants & Dorset 'Bristol' double-decker climbs the bank to take it over the railway bridge and past Eastleigh Works. *Roy Panting*

'Lord Nelson' class 4-6-0 No. 30861 *Lord Anson* runs into Southampton Central at the head of a Waterloo-Bournemouth train during August 1953, looking sadly in need of a clean. *E.R. Morten*

Southampton Central's splendid clock towers above BR Standard class '5MT' 4-6-0 No. 73082 on a Weymouth Quay-Waterloo train, September 1965. *Real Photographs*

This was the first time I had worked on a 'WD' 2-8-0 and at the time I sincerely hoped it would be the last. However, I did work on many more but never again did I have any problems with them, as they proved to be good free steaming engines providing the fuel was anything that resembled coal!

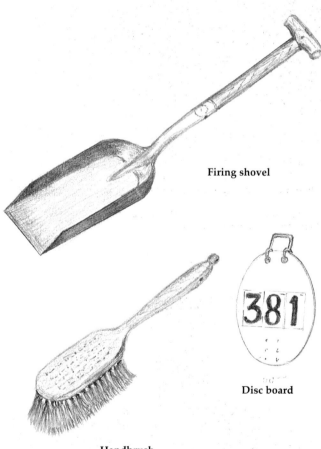

Firing shovel

Disc board

Handbrush

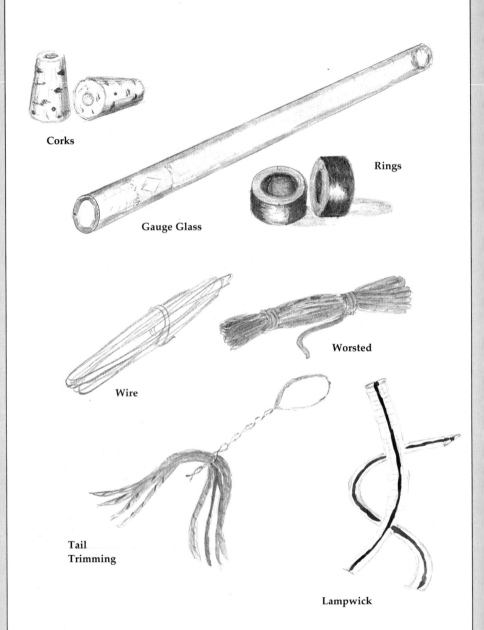

Corks

Gauge Glass

Rings

Wire

Worsted

Tail
Trimming

Lampwick

Chapter Three

The Tricks of the Trade

The War years brought many hardships, also much damage to locomotives, track and buildings, but it was a time of compassion and comradeship that sadly has not been the same since. Many railwaymen were pushed almost to the limits of their endurance having to work long hours, then often putting in a stint as a Home Guard, a Firewatcher, an Air Raid Warden or other volunteer work, but they always managed to keep cheerful in the best traditions of the British race.

I was still with Bill Smith when the War ended and working conditions slowly improved. The stations again had lights, which was something I had not seen in six years of War and the state of our locomotives also improved as materials again became available. The drab paint schemes were replaced with the beautiful Southern Green which was a joy to behold but the brass plates on the sides of the cabs were gone never to return.

Bill and I always kept the footplate of No. 106 spotlessly clean and the fireirons were kept in tip-top condition for use as they were intended, namely to clean the fire and seldom, if ever, for the purpose of correcting a fault in it. Whenever we had time I would run the tubes with a rod that we kept specially on the top of the driver's side tank to ensure that No. 106 maintained her free steaming qualities. I would also paint the disc boards carried by all Southern Railway locomotives which were used to give the signalmen an indication of route to be taken.

Whilst I was busy at these tasks, Bill would check the trimmings or perhaps change a gauge glass if he considered it necessary, rather than wait until one burst, which could well be at an awkward moment.

My next move was back up into No. 2 Link, but this time I was rostered with driver Syd Adams, so again it was necessary to establish a good working partnership. This was not so easy in this Link as we had lots of spare turns and we were often separated, having to cover holidays and sickness which could mean working in No. 1 Link or, indeed, any other for that matter. I never did like spare turns because often long hours were spent sitting in the dingy mess room and the time always went slowly, especially if there was no one else with whom to converse.

I knew that it could not be too long before I had to sit for my driving exam so, I often made use of the enforced idleness to make sure I knew all that was required of me. In fact, I learned a lot more than was expected of me, but I never regretted it because it proved so useful to me in the ensuing years. Time has taught me though that it is not always the man with the most knowledge that makes the best driver, but in most cases that rule does apply.

Right from the start I realised that Syd was quite a different type of driver to my previous mate, but I soon adjusted to his style of driving. I had to work harder because he did work the engines more heavily, but I did manage to keep pace with him except on one occasion when we worked a special to Waterloo and were booked to take the engine to Nine Elms, dispose of it, then travel back to Bournemouth 'on the cushions'. On arrival at Waterloo we were met by the running foreman who asked us if we would work the 3.30 pm to Bournemouth as the rostered Nine Elms men were required to work a Boat Train Special to Southampton, conveying passengers bound for the United States. We were, of course, only too happy to oblige as it meant that we would receive extra mileage payment and would arrive home much earlier than we had expected.

The locomotive for the 3.30 pm was a 'King Arthur' class No. 755 *The Red Knight* which differed from the rest of that class in its valves and it had a large chimney to go with its multiple blast pipe, which gave it quite a 'bark'. The best way to work this locomotive was to give her plenty of regulator but to pull the lever up into 15 per cent cut-off, then she would run a train without difficulty and in a very economical manner.

I mentioned this fact to Syd as I had been in conversation with a Nine Elms driver only a few days before when he had, in fact, worked the 3.30 pm down himself. He had explained this engine's features to me, mentioning the best way to handle the locomotive which was the pride and joy of the Nine Elms Shed Master, Mr Maitland. He took a special interest in No. 755 making sure that it was maintained in tip-top condition to work this particular train which, although it was lightly loaded, had a good number of stops and was fairly sharply timed.

We left Waterloo right on time, but Syd worked the engine in his usual manner which was full regulator with the lever around 40 per cent cut-off and although I put the injector on before we reached Vauxhall, I found that the water level was falling instead of being maintained as it should have been. The steam pressure was well up approaching Wimbledon with the water level down to half a glass. I pointed out the position to Syd and then put his side injector on as well, but even this did not seem to show any improvement in the boiler content.

With both injectors on, the boiler pressure started to fall and we ran into Woking, which was our first stop, with only an inch of water in the glass, 120 pounds pressure on the clock but four minutes before time. I shut off the driver's side injector and the steam pressure started to rise immediately, which showed that there was no fault in my fire. With the two minutes allowed at the station, plus the four minutes early arrival, I filled the boiler and she was almost over to blowing off point when we got the 'right away' from the guard so I gave Syd the tip and we were on our way. Again over went the regulator, up came the lever to 40 per cent and we were blasting away again so on went the injector at once. Before we reached Purbright Junction we were back to half a glass of water, so I had no alternative but to put on the second injector.

The rate that the water fell slowed, but still it continued. Then the steam pressure started to fall as we were, obviously, working the locomotive beyond capacity so I again I drew Syd's attention to our plight saying, 'Its no good Syd we are getting very low on water, both injectors are on, there is nothing more that I can do, we will have to stop for a "blow up"'. No sooner had I said this than the brake started to go on as we did not have enough steam to maintain 21 inches of vacuum. Sid closed the regulator and we ran to a stand half way between Farnborough and Fleet, then as soon as we had half a glass of water I shut off both injectors and was gratified to see the steam pressure rapidly building up.

As soon as we had 180 lb. pressure, Syd blew the whistle and we were again in motion, with the regulator being pushed open to full, then, as the lever was being pulled up, the thought went through my mind, 'Here we go again!', but this time Syd pulled the lever up to 15 per cent which brought about an incredible change in our previous situation. With the steam gauge over to almost 200 lb. pressure, I put on my injector, but this time the water level not only held, it did, in fact, start to rise slowly.

I was very impressed by the locomotive's performance and despite the fact that we had stoppd for about 2 minutes, we ran into Basingstoke right on time. After we came to a stand Syd said, 'I should have taken notice of what you told me. I thought I knew better but it is never too late to learn'. The rest of the journey gave us no further problems, Syd making sure to pull the lever well up as soon as possible after leaving a station.

I made a mental note after this incident to listen to the advice of others and not to dismiss their friendly words of wisdom without, at least, giving them a try first. It has often been said that we learn something new each day and we both most certainly did on that occasion.

I worked with Syd for 2½ years but I never became close to him as I had with previous mates. Maybe it was because I always had the feeling that he looked down on firemen for reasons best known to himself, but he trusted me to do my work and never questioned my method of firing. When we were spare I took on jobs that were given to Syd, such as packing regulator glands, changing gauge glasses or renewing trimmings, just to while away the time and also to gain experience in doing these jobs which most drivers disliked intensely, Syd included.

It was during this period in No. 2 Link that I experienced the worst day's work I ever had when I was booked up in No. 1 Link for a London trip with driver Bert Whittle. We were to work the 8.46 am from Bournemouth to Waterloo on No. 35028 *Clan Line* which was Bert's own engine. This train stopped at all stations to Brockenhurst then Lyndhurst, Totton, Southampon, St Denys, Eastleigh, Winchester, Basingstoke, Woking and Waterloo, and consisted of eight coaches, which was a very light load for No. 35028.

The fireman I relieved had built up a good fire and had given the cab a thorough clean up so everything pointed to an easy day's work for me. No. 35028 was steaming freely and I had to keep the firehole door well open to stop her from lifting the safety valves, so I sat down to take it easy. Then, as we were pulling away from Hinton Admiral station, a gauge glass literally exploded sending boiling water in all directions and filling the cab with steam. The Klinger type gauge glasses fitted to these locomotives had no restrictor valves and the cocks to shut them off were too small, making it very difficult to operate them.

I reached out to close the firehole door, but my hand was scalded by the water that was cascading down so I used the shovel to close the door, then put the injector on quickly as we were, obviously, losing water. I crossed the footplate to make sure Bert was all right as I could not see him, so I reached out and touched his shoulder, shouting out, 'Are you OK?'.

'Yes, I am all right, we will make New Milton then deal with it', he replied.

On arrival there it was soon obvious that we could not close the cocks on the gauge glass unless we reduced the boiler pressure. So, securing the locomotive, Bert opened the cylinder cocks, then opened the regulator to get rid of some steam. I closed the dampers and put on the second injector as I had no way of knowing how much water was in the boiler. Also it would help to reduce steam pressure.

Bert sat on the shovelling plate with his coat over his head to protect him from the hot water and then directed a jet of water from the 'pep pipe' into the fire to reduce its heat while I went back to explain the situation to the guard and the station master, then requested the signalman to inform control of our predicament. I asked the station master if he had anything to cover my hands so that I could make an attempt to close the gauge glass cocks. He gave me some sacks, also the signalman lent me an oilskin mac, so, donning it, I then wrapped my hands and arms and made my way back to the footplate. Bert was still spraying the fire with water and by now was soaking wet, but still sitting there patiently with water dripping down all around him.

I suggested that he should get some air while I had a go at the gauge glass cocks, so as soon as he was off the locomotive I took the shovel and by guiding the blade up under the cocks I did, after three attemps, manage to close them, only to find that it was the wrong side that I had isolated. Not to be daunted I turned my attention to the other glass and after a struggle I closed the steam and water cocks, then opened the drain cock but not before my hands had become badly scalded, although my face had escaped injury.

The steam quickly cleared and to our relief the glass had shut off as tight as a bottle. We took stock of our situation, which was not at all encouraging, but almost as soon as the damper was opened the fire started to burn up and we had a full glass of water. 'Give us about 10 or so minutes and we should be on our way', said Bert to the station master and true to his word we were, indeed, on the move. On arrival at Brockenhurst we were met by the station foreman who informed us that there would be a standby locomotive at Southampton if we required one. Bert thanked him adding, 'My mate's hands are badly scalded, will you get someone to bandage them when we arrive there'. Assuring us that he would he gave the 'right away', relaying it from the guard. Then turning on his heels he went straight to the telephone to send the message.

Bert asked me if I was OK to work on and I assured him that I was and we there and then decided that we would keep No. 35028 and get the Klinger water glass changed at Nine Elms. As we were approaching Redbridge, to our dismay the good gauge glass started to spurt water and steam, so we shut it off as quickly as possible, but again the task was far from easy.

We had plenty of water in the boiler, so we were in no danger, but I put on the injector just to be on the safe side, shutting if off as we ran into Southampton, so we now had no choice but to change engines.

Two ambulance men were waiting on the platform and stepped forward asking, 'Where is the casualty, we have an ambulance waiting outside'. I at once assured them that I did not require hospital treatment, but would appreciate bandages to cover my hands to keep the heat of the fire off them as they were very painful.

A police officer heard my request, so he offered to bandage my hands if they would give him the correct dressings which they readily did.

Bert said he would change the engines whilst I was being attended to and he was soon back on the train with a decripit looking 'S15' that had been out in service since the early hours on a freight train to Southampton docks. The fire was low and, obviously, in need of a clean, but I soon placed coal all around the firebox to bring the boiler pressure up while Bert coupled on having kindly volunteered to do so.

I had to work very hard to make the 'S15' steam, resorting to the use of the fireirons on several occasions, which had a disastrous effect on my bandages, ripping them to shreds.

The coal was well back in the tender and I had to keep dragging it forward to a more accessible position, but despite the adversities we eventually arrived at Waterloo about 30 minutes late. Our return train, the 3.20 pm down was a fairly fast one and the 'S15' was totally unsuitable for it so Bert requested something more able to do the job. We were given 'King Arthur' class No. 777, *Sir Lamiel*, and informed that it had been prepared so Bert told me to go and get my hands re-dressed by the appointed first aid attendant. On my way to see him I removed the remains of the bandages to save time, but he tore me off a strip, telling me I should have kept my hands covered. However, when he saw how badly they were torn he set to work to replace them, impressing on me the need to keep the burns clean.

When I returned, Bert was busy trying to get some life into the fire, because the fireman who had made the fire up had filled the firebox with small coal and it looked in a very sorry state. With time running short we set off for Waterloo, but had not managed to get a full head of steam when it was time to leave. Again it was necessary to use the fireirons in order to try to make the engine steam which was not only arduous but very painful. It was mostly due to Bert's superb handling of the locomotive, making full use of his excellent knowledge of the road by using every slight downgrade to our advantage, that we kept time as well as we did. No matter how hard I tried I could not get any life into the front of the fire. Then I noticed water streaming down the tubeplate from leaking tubes. The whole of the journey was a constant battle to make ends meet but, between us we managed the task, although at the end of it I was dog tired and my hands were extremely painful, with the dressings again in tatters. I made out an accident report then went home to a good meal and, very soon, in the good company of my wife, I felt a whole lot better.

After several more incidents with the Klinger gauge glasses, they were fitted with restrictor valves and longer cock handles fitted to make them easier to close. Eventually they were replaced by the ordinary type glasses which could be changed by the driver in a very short space of time. They were easier to see and in the event of breakage could be shut off quickly and without danger.

Syd and I had a special one day when we had to ride 'passenger' up to Brockenhurst and relieve a train which consisted of six coaches, two of them

Pullman cars, provided for the Ministry of Transport to carry out an inspection of sidings that were specially built for wartime use. These were at Ringwood, Holmsley, Wimborne and West Moors on the 'Old Road' having been used for military supplies as well as large quantities of petrol and oil.

We made a brief stop at Holmsley just to examine one siding, then were off again to Ringwood where a further inspection was made. We filled the tender of our 'T9' locomotive No. 119 with water and I shovelled some coal forward for the journey back to London. After about half an hour, we left for West Moors where the MOT officials were booked to have a meal, which was provided by the Pullman dining car staff. As we were scheduled to stay there for two hours, I decided to clean the fire and was just starting when our guard came up to the engine saying, 'They have laid out a lunch for you and your mate, so leave that and come on back to the dining car now, or it will get cold!' Syd was oiling the engine, so I passed on the message to him, but much to my surprise he said, 'I don't want their lunch. You can go if you want to'. I immediately downed tools, and made my way back to the dining car. Here the steward showed me to a compartment where a table had been set for two. He asked where Syd was and when I told him he said, 'What's the matter with him, does he want to spoil it for everyone else'. All I could say was, 'He's like that' so he told me to eat both lunches if I felt like it.

The lunch was so good, consisting of beautiful roast pork, baked potatoes and three veg that I did just that, as I could not see it go to waste because we were sill on rations and food was far from plentiful. After eating a large helping of dessert, I thanked the steward and then went back to the engine where Syd was eating his cheese sandwiches. He was non-committal when I told him what I had been given.

I cleaned the fire and made it up again after Syd had finished his snack, then after the sidings had been inspected we left for Wimborne where we made a 10 minute stop. With the job completed, we took the train as far as Southampton via Poole and Bournemouth this time. Relief was waiting for us at Southampton so I took the water pipe that the driver offered up to me, and filled the tender up again, this time with sufficient water to take them back to Waterloo.

Syd and I made a good work team, always well on top of the job but as I have said before, sadly lacking in that all important close link which made life so much more enjoyable.

With summer fast approaching I had good reason to believe that my spell with Syd would not last much longer because by now I was the second most senior fireman in No. 2 Link and I could expect a move up at any time to the Main Line gang, with its more social hours and additional pay.

In May 1949 I finally reached the top of the tree as a fireman when I was put into No. 1 Link for the summer along with driver Frank Carter on 'Merchant Navy' class No. 35027 *Port Line*. I had worked with lots of really good drivers but I was to experience the joy of working with a man who, in my opinion, was in a class of his own, for he took the art of driving to its very highest pinnacle.

He did it with a skill that was almost beyond understanding because he never looked at his watch but would pass junctions and timing points dead on time using the absolute minimum of coal and water. He was over 60, with an easy, cheerful way that never varied no matter what time of day it was, or what event occurred, however stressful it might be.

He had supreme confidence in himself and in me, I am happy to say. Never once did he question or interfere in anything that I did, which made for a happy working relationship that would be difficult to surpass. We had in No. 35027 an engine second to none and we took a great pride in keeping her in tip-top condition with the footplate spotlessly clean and brass, copper and steelwork positively gleaming. The cab paintwork was a buff colour and this was clean enough to eat your dinner off, with even the roof shining. Tender lockers were lined with paper and the gullies for the fireirons were always kept absolutely free of coal, making them readily available, not that I ever had need of them except for cleaning the fire.

In Frank's capable hands I could always finish firing as we passed Winchester on our way to Waterloo, then after giving the floor a washdown, I used to get out the 'Brasso' and polish the brasswork as well as the copper pipes, finishing off by scouring the steelwork with fine emery cloth to occupy the time. Few locomotives had as much pipework on the footplate nor such large brass boxes containing axlebox oil which, when polished never failed to bring compliments from anyone seeing it.

These engines had 6,000 gallon tenders and Frank would never take water at Southampton on the up journey saying, 'It's a waste of time, we won't use it anyway', which was so true because we invariably had over 3,000 gallons left on arrival at Waterloo.

He would not take water at Waterloo as it was a troublesome procedure because it was necessary to move twice owing to the high tender ladders, which prevented the pipe from being pulled round. We would fill the tender on the corner of the shed at Nine Elms just before we left and that was ample to get us back to Bournemouth but, if the locomotive was going through to Weymouth we would top up with water at Southampton.

Frank was the only driver with whom I worked who did not take water at Southampton on the up journey, and I recall one incident which goes to illustrate this man's ability.

For the whole of one week 'Lord Nelson' class No. 30865 *Sir John Hawkins* was on the 12.40 pm from Bournemouth to Waterloo with the sole purpose to establish if these locomotives could be used on non-stop trains between these two stations. We had the job on the last day and when we had filled the tender at Bournemouth, a CM&EE official was on hand to check the precise amount with a dipstick.

When we stopped at Southampton he was on hand again and was more than a little concerned when we made no move to put the pipe in. He asked Frank, 'Why are you not taking water?' to which Frank replied, 'Because we don't need it!'

'But I need it for my records', explained the official, so Frank said, 'My mate will stick the pipe in if you care to pull it round for him' but he made no attempt to do so himself.

The pipe was pulled round and the tender duly filled, again being tested with the dipstick before and after filling, then it was time to leave. Arriving at Waterloo dead on time, the water was again checked, then the dumbfounded CM&EE man showed us his set of figures saying, 'It's incredible but you have used 1,000 gallons less than the nearest man to you and less than half as much as the worst!'

The check had shown that we still had well over half a tender of water left but Frank did not disclose that No. 30865 had been his regular engine before No. 35027 and he knew it like the back of his hand.

It was the same story when we went to Oxford. We took on water at Basingstoke only in each direction and it was never necessary for me to shovel coal forward at Oxford for the return journey, so lightly did Frank work the engine.

On many occasions when drivers were learning the road with us to London, specially on the down journey, they would comment to me, 'Frank's never timing this train, working the loco like that'. To which I would always say, 'Check the time at Worting Junction and I'll bet that we will be right on the dot', and we always were. One driver asked me how Frank did it without looking at his watch but I could only reply, 'That I will never know, it is a mystery to me too!'

During early June I had to go in for my driving examination in company with fireman Bill Hayward who was one above me in seniority. I had no fears about passing because of Walt Churchill's earlier tuition and the fact that I regularly attended Mutual Improvement classes run by the men themselves. Here on occasions, I used to take my turn at teaching because I have always been absorbed in the technical side of steam locomotives and diesels as well for that matter. I have also had a keen interest in rules and regulations which has served me in good stead over the years.

Both Bill and I passed without difficulty and very soon afterwards I had my first driving turn which was a Special from London to Swanage. The 'Merchant Navy' class engine that worked the train down from Waterloo came off at Bournemouth Central, as they were not permitted on the Swanage branch and we set back on the train of nine coaches with 'Q' class locomotive No. 30541. It is strange, but doing the job as a driver was totally different from driving with the driver on the footplate and I felt on edge, not at all like my usual self.

When we had the 'right away' I opened up the regulator and was really making the sparks fly, being fearful of losing time, carrying on like this until we reached Poole 2 minutes early, when it suddenly occurred to me that this certainly was not the way that Frank would be doing he job. Then thinking of him, I felt an inner calm and every trace of tension was gone, so from then on I worked 30541 in a completely different manner.

I found that running the train to time presented no problems, much, I am sure, to the relief of my fireman Stan Ireson.

From that day on, every time I was out driving, I always managed to do so in a calm easy way very reminiscent of Frank's attitude to the job, refusing to be ruffled, no matter what the situation was.

One Saturday Frank and I were on at 8.30 am to work the 8.46 to Waterloo, returning with the 2.30 pm fast to Bournemouth, which meant a fairly quick turnround at Nine Elms. So, as usual, I lifted the clinker at Waterloo, standing it in the centre of the fire grate ready to throw out at the depot, then placed hand picked lumps of coal in the back corners of the firebox to give me a good foundation to work with when I had got rid of the clinker, which I did as soon as we reached the depot. This only took a few minutes with the special shovel I kept locked to the fireiron bracket. This was the blade of a GWR coal shovel, with its extraordinary capacity, fitted with a hickory shunting pole handle which I used solely for throwing out dead clinker and it was an ideal tool.

I now made up the fire, making sure that the centre was all good sized lumps, avoiding using small coal for this purpose, continuing until the firebox was full to capacity, with Frank's approval as he was in favour of a good box of fire.

As we were about to leave Nine Elms a pair of Bournemouth men asked for a lift to Waterloo so that they could ride home passenger on our train and the fireman, Jack Stockley, said to me, 'I have not worked on one of these locos, how do you fire to them?' I offered advice saying, 'What ever you do Jack, don't put any more fire in the box than I have got now, then put a sprinkle on now and then, but don't overdo it!' The Ajax firedoor was almost closed so Jack took a look to check just how how much fire I had in the firebox, which I will admit was above the rim of the firehole.

He looked at me in amazement saying, 'She won't steam like that, you will be busy using the dart and pricker to get steam!' I assured him, 'I won't need the fireirons and it is very unlikely that I shall need the coal shovel. Ride down with us and see for yourself!'

Still far from convinced, Jack declined the offer saying, 'No, I'll keep out of the way and ride in the train'.

On leaving Waterloo No. 35027 responded at once and I had to ease down the damper as well as opening the firehole door slightly to keep her under control. With Frank in his usual form, I sat down most of the way to Southampton, getting up only to adjust the injector when it was needed. On arrival there Jack got out of the train and started to pull the water crane around when Frank stopped him saying, 'Don't waste your time with that, we have plenty of water!' So Jack put the chain back on the hook and came up onto the footplate to see how we had got on. At once I said, 'Jack you were right I've had a struggle all the way down, but only trying to keep her from blowing off, and now I am going to make sure if I need that sprinkle of coal I mentioned at Nine Elms'. Jack glanced up at the coal in the tender and it was exactly as we had left London because I had not once touched the shovel, nor did I for the rest of the journey.

Many who read this will doubt my words but Jack will verify it without question and in the passing years has often mentioned it as, indeed, has Alex Saunders, another Bournemouth driver who also witnessed this phenomenon.

When we were on duties that did not involve London work, we did a mixed freight and passenger duty round the 'Old Road', a shunting turn at Bournemouth West, Branksome and Parkstone; also a mixed turn between Bournemouth and Eastleigh. This involved working a freight train from Bournemouth Central Goods Yard at 1.40 pm calling at Christchurch, shunting out the empty wagons there, then picking up the freshly loaded ones and taking the lot to Bevois Park Goods Yard where we unhooked, taking the engine on to Eastleigh Depot where we disposed of it. We then walked up to Eastleigh station, relieving the 5.30 pm from Waterloo, then working it on to Bournemouth Central where we had relief.

On these three turns Frank let me do most of the driving but I always did the firing as well in between shunts, although Frank would look after the water in the boiler, putting on the injector as needed.

On the 'Old Road' turn after we arrived at Wimborne we shunted out the yard then worked a passenger train to Poole, leaving the train there and running light to Bournemouth Shed. On the other three days of the late turn we worked in turn the 2.40 pm up to Waterloo, back with the 7.30 pm down, the 12.40 pm up, back with the 6.30 pm down and the 11.02 am up, back with the 4.35 pm down, later named the 'Royal Wessex'.

The early shift consisted of five turns; the 8.46 am up and down with the 3.20 pm; the 8.40 am up and back with the 1.30 pm; the 9.30 up Birkenhead train to Oxford and return and two Weymouth turns. On arrival at Bournemouth with the up Weymouth trains we were relieved by our opposite mates who then worked either the 2.40 p.m or the 12.40 pm to Waterloo.

When on these Weymouth turns we always made sure that the tender was fully coaled after the fire had been made up and on arrival at Bournemouth we made sure to have a good box of fire, a clean footplate, polished brass and copper to make it as easy as possible for our relief driver, Fred Perkins and fireman, Fred Christopher. It goes without saying that they did the same for us.

We were working the 12.40 pm up one Tuesday and had just been given the 'right away' at Southampton, so Frank eased No. 35027 away in his usual style, but when he tried to pull the reversing lever up there was a bad steam blow from underneath the engine and nothing happened. It was soon evident that the steam pipe to the reversing cylinder had broken and there was no way to shorten the travel of the valves. Most drivers would have stopped at Eastleigh for another engine, but not Frank, he just kept going, he did, however, work the regulator even easier than was his norm and much to his credit we arrived at Waterloo on time, with the only evidence of our plight showing itself in the fact that the cylinders were hotter than usual and the grease and oil on the ends of them had melted away, leaving them quite clean. A crackling sound came from them that was very reminiscent of frying bacon but devoid of that delicious aroma.

We had to be towed to Nine Elms as we had no means of reversing No. 35027 but, on arrival there the fitters soon replaced the broken steam pipe so that we were able to keep her for our return 6.30 pm down which was non-stop to Southampton then Bournemouth.

It was on the same 6.30 pm down that we had another incident which helps to demonstrate Frank's ability to cope with any situation. We were just passing through Vauxhall when there was an instantaneous bad blow from the front of the left cylinder each time the steam was admitted to that end, which meant we were losing power but only by one sixth. It is true that this did impair Frank's vision somewhat but it was daylight and I made certain that I did not miss any signals, calling them out to Frank as soon as I sighted them.

When we arrived at Southampton, Frank went round to find out what was wrong, then came back to the footplate saying, 'That big nut is missing off of the front of the cylinder!' Completely mystified by this statement I went round and had a look for myself then realized that Frank's 'big nut' was, in fact, the compression relief valve that we had lost, which, of course, left a sizeable hole in the front cylinder cover. Frank's one failing was that he was not at all mechanically minded and, although he could work any locomotive to perfection, I sometimes had to remind him of the names of the parts or book defects which I was happy to do.

The summer of 1949 was, for me, perfection in every way, the weather was excellent, working with Frank was an absolute joy and No. 35027 was, in my humble opinion, the best locomotive ever built. But, as the saying goes, 'all good things come to an end' because the end of September meant that I had to part company with Frank. Although he has long since passed away, I shall never forget him and the time we spent together, such was the impression he made upon me.

I resolved to model my way of driving on Frank's, but only my firemen in later years can testify as to whether I achieved my aim. It certainly was not through lack of trying.

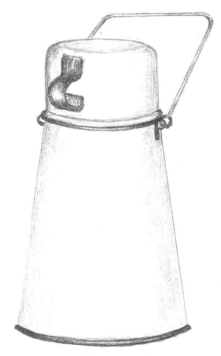

Tea can

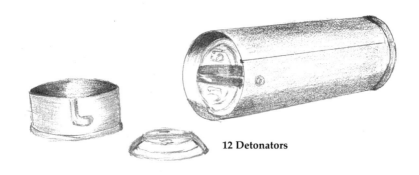

12 Detonators

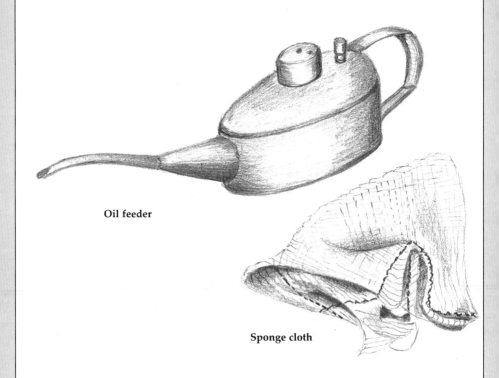

Oil feeder

Sponge cloth

Chapter Four

Senior Fireman

I thought that I would have to go back into No. 2 Link but, luckily for me, two extra drivers were required at Bournemouth and that meant that I stayed in No. 1 Link but now had a different driver, Syd Futcher; also another locomotive which was No. 35030. Syd was a comparitive stranger to me because I had seldom worked with him, so it was with a degree of uncertainty that I started off my first week's work with him.

Our first day together was a London trip and No. 35030 had just been fitted with a new multiple blast pipe cap of smaller diameter by way of an experiment. We had a CM&EE technician riding with us to study the behaviour of the loco and a gauge had been fitted to measure the vacuum created in the smokebox. The pull on the fire was greater but this had no effect on the steaming qualities of No. 35030 and all went well until we had passed Eastleigh, then the steam pressure started to fall for no apparent reason. Putting on the blower failed to have any effect and desperate efforts by me still did not bring about any marked improvement. However, when Syd shut off the steam for the flyover at Worting the sudden increase in pressure was proof that there was no fault with my firing, but as soon as Syd opened the regulator again, back it went.

With the easy running from Worting Junction to Waterloo, it was possible to shut off frequently so we did not suffer any loss of time but the CM&EE technician was unable to offer any explanation as to the engine's erratic behaviour. I was not at all happy about this first trip with Syd, so as soon as we arrived at Waterloo I went round to the front of the engine and opened the smokebox to try to establish the cause.

Much to my surprise the smokebox was devoid of ash and the main steam pipe joint packing from both pipes was laying on the floor of the smokebox. The CM&EE man had followed me and he said, 'Well there is the answer, the steam from those joints has been preventing her from steaming with the regulator open. It also explains why she came over as soon as your mate shut off. You will have to have another loco back'.

Syd was a bit disgruntled about having to leave No. 35030 at Nine Elms, but there was no alternative, so we had to make do with 'Lord Nelson' class No. 30863 which, I am pleased to say, could not have responded better, giving us a perfect return trip.

Two days later, when we arrived at Nine Elms we were told that No. 35030 had been repaired and that we could have her back again. The CM&EE man was on hand again when we attached to our down 4.35 pm train at Waterloo and he told us that the joints had been replaced. This time the joints held until the pull up towards Purbright Junction, then it was a repeat of our previous trip, with the packing blown out of both side main steam pipe joints. At Bournemouth she was stopped again.

We were informed the next day that No. 35030 was to be sent to Stewarts

Lane Depot to work the 'Golden Arrow' train from Victoria to Dover and the rest of our 'Merchant Navy' locomotives were to follow in due course. We were promised new 'West Country' class locomotives as replacements and this brought a storm of protests from No. 1 Link men as we were proud of, and delighted with, our 'Packets'.

The protests were of no avail so Syd and I were given 'Battle of Britain' class 34055 *Fighter Pilot* which, in company with No. 34054 was loaned to Bournemouth by Salisbury depot. On our first trip on this smaller engine we were very impressed with her performance as, indeed, were our opposite mates, driver Syd Friend and fireman Ted Hill. This engine was fitted with a drop grate which was a great asset to the firemen and saved a lot of hard work. She was also very free steaming. We had expected to find a vast difference in the speed and pulling of this locomotive, but this was not the case. She handled all trains with ease, showing only slightly less performance when faced with steep banks such as Weymouth and Parkstone.

Syd and I soon built up a rapport that would have been difficult to surpass, liking and trusting each other in a way that was more akin to father and son than driver and fireman, and we eagerly awaited news of our promised new 'West Country'. The day arrived after a month when, with some regret, we lost 34055 but we soon realised that we had gained in many ways when our new 'West Country' class No. 34093 *Saunton* arrived.

With her larger tender, wider cab, brand new condition and beautifully balanced drop grate, which could be opened with one hand, she was a gem. I soon had her new brass and copper work looking a picture with every part polished to perfection. Her unmarked paintwork was so smooth that little effort was required to keep it looking just like enamel plate.

Two other 'West Country' class locomotives followed closely after but neither of them was as good as No. 34093. No. 34094's drop grate was a swine to open and No. 34095, although strong, did not have the absolutely free steaming qualities of *Saunton* or 'Saunter On' as Syd delighted to call her. This batch of locomotives were fitted with dampers making them more controllable than the earlier ones, which was a great advantage.

The winter of 1949 was one with quite a few fogs but it presented Syd and me with very few problems. It was a fact, strange but true, that on the up journey, the steam from the chimney tended to drop down over the fireman's side of the cab but the reverse was the case on the down journey.

On murky days I would endeavour to make up my fire with Welsh coal at Nine Elms, often not taking coal there as in those days it was always Yorkshire 'Hard Black' which, although excellent, tended to be smokey.

On passing Hampton Court Junction on the down journey when we started to encounter semaphore signals, I would check them, then call them out to Syd, who would acknowledge them with a circular wave of a sponge cloth. I would then place six shovelfuls of coal around the firebox, close the firehole door then sit down and look out for the next signals, again calling out to Syd when I saw they were clear.

This was repeated signal after signal until we approached the distant signal for Wooton, then I would tell Syd he would have to find it as it was a low one and, therefore, not visible from the fireman's side of the footplate owing to the curve.

When he had located it Syd would often say, 'That is the first one I have seen since we passed Hampton Court Junction' and I am sure it was true, which clearly demonstrates the absolute trust he had in me.

I could not help overhearing a remark made by Nine Elms driver Jerry Sartin on a particularly foggy day to Syd at Waterloo, 'It is on a day like this that you can do with a good Fireman' to which Syd replied 'Jerry, I have got one, in fact, there is none better!' I pretended not to hear but I have got to admit it filled me with pride to be regarded in that way!

There is nothing more satisfying than to have a trip to London with the steam gauge seemingly glued to the 280 lb. mark and the water bobbing just under the top nut the whole of the way, and with No. 34093, every day was such an event. We never had a bad trip nor an anxious moment when we were together but one day I had leave and Syd had to stop for a 'blow up' on our Oxford turn. The next day I asked him what had happened and he replied, 'The Fireman let me down, it just would not have happened if you had been there!'

When we went to London or Oxford we would always go to the canteen together and would often cycle home in each other's company as we lived near to one another. Syd gave me a free hand to fire in my own way and I adopted a system of cleaning the fire at Waterloo making full use of the drop grate fitted to 34093. On arrival there I would throw the fire into the back corners of the firebox, then dart up the exposed clinker, placing it on the drop grate, extinguish it with the flexible water pipe, then drop it down into the ashpan closing the door afterwards. I would then run the pricker through the back half of the firebox, pulling any clinker out and again placing it on the door.

I would repeat the process and after re-closing the drop grate, would start to make up the fire by placing lumps of coal under the firehole door and in the back corners, not bothering to push the fire over to cover the area of the drop grate. By the time we had left Waterloo to go to Nine Elms I usually had a good bed of fire which, on the run down there, would spread quickly to the rest of the firebox giving me a good start to build a really good box of fire.

I was always a firm believer in a large fire for Bulleid's locomotives and, providing the centre of the grate area was kept free of small coal, it never failed. Both Syd and Frank were much in favour of this method because of the fact that these excellent locomotives responded so well to it.

These engines were fitted with an automatic water treatment system and could be blown down from the cab by the use of two steam cocks. A clock to record the time and duration of each blow down was fitted and this provided a printed record on a circular card which would last for one week. On the up journey we were instructed to blow down for 30 seconds at Woodfidley Crossing, Allbrook and Fleet with a final one on the pit at Nine Elms.

This blow down almost cost me my life one day at Nine Elms because we were late arriving there through a signal failure and, as was usual in these circumstances, I was given assistance to trim the coal in the tender. Having made up my fire, I went underneath to rake out the ashpan entering the pit from the rear of the engine, just in time to see Syd climbing out of the pit after oiling the bogies. I had just started to rake out when I heard the top steam cock of the blow down opening so, knowing that the exit nozzle was immediately above my head, I dropped the rake I was using and ran towards the front of the engine.

Steam, boiling water and ash shot along the pit but I managed to miss most of it, in a burst of speed that would have left even Ben Johnson standing. The steam took my breath away and I admit I was shaking with fright when I climbed back on to the footplate. So, turning to Syd who had just closed the blow down I said, 'You nearly had me then Syd, I was underneath when you blew her down!' in a voice far from steady.

Syd was absolutely horrified, saying, 'Sorry Stan, I thought you were up there on the tender, I shouted up to tell you I would blow her down to save time!' Syd was clearly shocked by what had happened adding, 'That's the first time I have used that damned contraption and believe me it's the last!'

I re-assured him saying, 'Don't worry Syd, no harm was done!' but my heart was bumping like a trip hammer.

I made sure never to go underneath again at Nine Elms, because I found I could rake out from the side of the locomotive using the pricker. I said no more about the incident to Syd but it was quite some time before I could calm down, so close had I been to being scalded to death.

Syd never touched the blow down again and he made doubly sure that no one was in the vicinity when I carried out this operation.

I worked with Syd for nine happy months, then it was time for him to retire and I well remember our last trip down which, although it was excellent, was tinged with sadness because we were such good mates.

After we had relief at Bournemouth, we walked along the platform and Syd stopped, then with tears trickling down his cheeks and his voice charged with emotion said, 'Stan I don't want to finish, if you could stay with me I would be happy to carry on till I'm 80!'

In those days footplate men had such an affinity with their work that it was not so much a job but more a way of life, arduous maybe, but so rewarding!

I missed Syd because when two men work so well together it was not easy to accept readily a new driver with such a different way of working the same locomotive. On No. 34093 the regulator worked so freely that when it was eased down after passing Hampton Court Junction it would often close altogether on its own, so Syd, to prevent this from happening, kept a wooden rail key in the locker and he would place it under the handle to stop it from closing. But on my first trip down with my new mate, Frank Horn, the regulator handle was up in the roof, touching the stop.

I told Frank about Syd's key but his response was, 'We have got to time the train mate'. However, I noticed that we were passing through Hersham when we should have just been passing Hampton Court!

Frank Horn was of a nervous disposition and it showed in the way he handled No. 34093 working her far heavier than Syd, but it was his way of driving so I had to adjust my firing to suit his style. I got on fairly well with Frank but must admit that I did resent having to burn so much more coal than I did with Frank Carter and Syd Futcher.

Frank would look a his watch every few minutes and this was usually accompanied by a little extra tug on the regulator so concerned was he about 'timing' a train. Frank would take water frequently and would never have dreamed of not filling the tender at Southampton in both directions, which was just as well because I am sure we used twice as much as Frank Carter did, therefore, we would never have made it!

Frank was a conscientious man and very well informed about the mechanical construction of a steam locomotive, making sure to book even the smallest defect, checking the next day to make certain it had been carried out.

Our new opposite mate, Bill Smith, had just requested No. 34108 *Wincanton* to replace No. 34093 as she had to be stopped for periodical examination. No. 34108 was new from shops and had just been allocated to Bournemouth, but she was not fitted with a drop grate, so cleaning the fire was more difficult. It was still possible to clean the fire at Waterloo, although Frank was fearful at first in case the ashpan should be damaged, but I proved conclusively to him that this was not the case which allayed his fears.

No. 34108 was a good locomotive, strong and free steaming, but not so good as No. 34093; or, maybe, I was prejudiced thinking of my good days with Syd!

Frank never at any time made any comments about my firing on London or Oxford turns, but he would make some irritating remark, such as 'put that lamp away' or 'drop that damper', which was quite unnecessary as I knew my job and did not need to be told. I resented it but he was the driver and I had to accept it, making no comment but sometimes I had to bite my tongue, although I soon forgot it.

We were on a Weymouth turn one day and when we stopped at Wareham we were opposite the water tank which was situated at the Dorchester end alongside the down bay road. An allotment was close to the tank and the permanent way ganger was standing at the end of it, lifting the leaves of a large bed of rhubarb with his hammer. Frank spotted the ruby sticks and said, 'Got any to spare mate?'

The ganger replied, 'Help yourself Driver', so Frank got off the footplate and picked a few sticks, then when invited to take more pulled a large bundle. Putting his hand in his pocket Frank offered the ganger a shilling saying, 'Thanks, get yourself a drink'; but much to Frank's consternation the ganger refused saying, 'No that's OK, it does not belong to me'.

I can still picture Frank standing there with that big bundle under his arm not knowing where to put his face, but we often laughed about it later, although it is true to say he never asked for 'more'.

I stayed with Frank during the summers of 1950 and 1951 but I was gradually climbing up the promotion ladder and was now the senior fireman in No. 1 Link. I knew that during 1952 I could be taken off for the summer at least to be available for driving turns which were sure to become more plentiful.

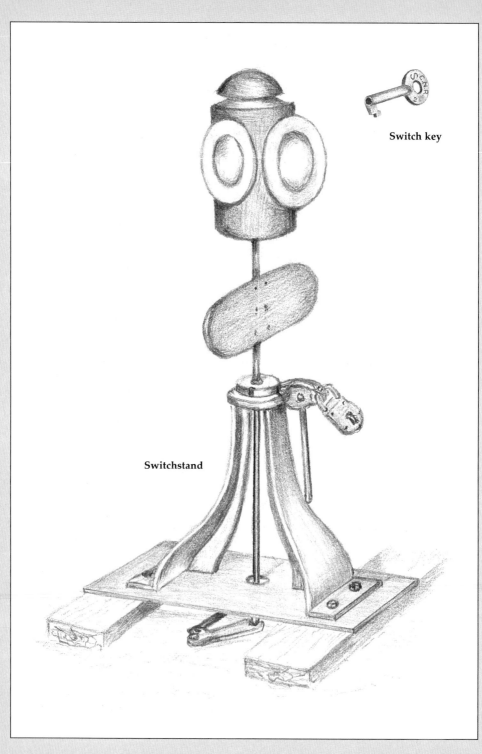

Switch key

Switchstand

Chapter Five

Canadian Caper

Early in 1952 my wife expressed a desire for a change and suggested that we should emigrate to Australia. Although I had always been content with my lot in this country, I agreed to find out more about it by going up to London on my first day off.

On arrival at Australia House, I was informed that the waiting list for married couples with children would be about 2 years so. Disappointed, I went along to New Zealand House only to be told that the waiting list was even longer and it seemed that they were more interested in single people anyway. Not to be daunted I went on to Canada House and asked the interviewer, 'How soon can I go to Canada?' He replied, 'You can go tomorrow if you like, but you have to pay for your own passage. We will help you find employment on arrival and we will also give you and your family a free medical examination which is necessary before you can go'.

He asked where in Canada I wanted to go and I told him that I thought Toronto would be the best place for us because it is rapidly expanding with a good percentage of English people there. I felt that we would be more at ease there than, say, Montreal which was predominantly French. He then advised me to go over to the Ontario Immigration Office where they would provide me with all the information that I needed, also arrange for our medical and assist me in every way possible to find a job.

True to his word, the staff there could not have been more helpful, giving me colour brochures, maps, details of housing, in fact, everything that I needed to know, together with forms to fill in which would be sent on to Toronto, so that they had all my details before I arrived.

Having gone through all the procedures necessary I booked a passage from Southampton to Quebec on the RMS *Samaria*, sailing on 5th June, 1952.

I wrote to both the Canadian Pacific and the Canadian National Railways asking about the possibility of a job as a fireman. I received a reply from both, very similar in content, telling me that, although they could not offer me a job by post, my application would be considered on merit when I arrived in Toronto.

I had second thoughts about going in case I could not find employment because I had a wife and two children to support. So I decided not to burn my bridges but to ask for four months unpaid leave from British Railways, thus protecting my position as a passed fireman, ensuring that my 13 years seniority would not be lost in the event of being unable to get a job.

I had been advised not to take my family with me, but to go alone as accommodation was difficult to locate, houses being expensive and hard to obtain.

Having taken all the precautions I could, I set sail on 5th June, into the 'unknown', sharing my cabin with a Scotsman and a Welshman and we had a very pleasant voyage. We arrived safely in Quebec at 1.0 am where we boarded a train to Toronto, only to find that the coach we were booked on must have dated from the Pioneer days, as it had wooden slatted seats with backs that could be moved to allow one to face in either direction. With a twelve hour journey in front of us we soon found out that it was virtually impossible to get comfortable in them and spent the night talking because sleep was out of the question.

The locomotive was a Canadian National class '6100' of enormous proportions compared to our 'Merchant Navy' class, having a tender holding 11,800 gallons of water and 18 tons of coal. It marched the train of 15 coaches away with comparative ease over the St Lawrence River bridge which is similar to the bridge over the Firth of Forth in Scotland, then on towards Montreal 150 miles away.

On arrival there I was surprised when the locomotive stopped under a coal hopper and took coal while the fireman cleaned the fire using the drop grate to let the clinker down into the ashpan. Here it was doused with water and finally finished up in the pit below. The tender was filled with water while the train was being swept clean, drinking water tanks filled, paper towels replaced and fresh supplies taken on board for the dining car. All this was carried out without the locomotive being detached.

After some 50 minutes we were again under way with 350 miles to go before we finally reached our destination, the Ontario lakeside city of Toronto.

We arrived at Union station, which was run by the Toronto Terminals Railway, a joint venture between the CNR and CPR at 1.0 pm on Saturday 13th June. I went straight to the Travellers' Aid Society to enquire after lodgings. They advised me, quite wisely, not to get permanent lodgings but to get a room for two nights. When I knew what part of the City I would work in I was to contact them again and they would give me an address as near to my work as possible to avoid unnecessary travelling.

I was on the doorstep of the Ontario Immigration Office when they opened at 9.0 am on the Monday morning. After a fairly short wait, I was shown to the room of the Employment Officer who, upon enquiring as to my home town, informed me that he was one of the Canadian Air Force men who had been in the Metropole in Bournemouth when it was bombed on that awful Sunday lunchtime and luckily had been uninjured.

He asked, 'Do you want to continue as a Railway Fireman?' to which I replied with a firm 'yes'. He then telephoned the CPR to see if there were any vacancies in that grade, but the only vacancy in the Motive Power Depot was for a Boilermaker's helper, which we would call a Boilersmith's mate. When he saw that I was disappointed he asked whether it would be possible to transfer if a fireman's job occurred. As they answered in the affirmative I accepted it because I had very little money at that time.

I was then directed to the CPR Roundhouse at the west side of the city where I was given a letter to see the company doctor that very evening for a medical, which I had no difficulty in passing. I was then instructed to start work at 11.0 pm the next day at the Roundhouse which was large, having 32 tracks or stalls as they called them.

The Travellers' Aid Society fixed me up with an address close to the Depot at

464 Beresford Avenue, the landlady being Mrs Davis, a kindly lady aged about 60 who made me welcome, gave me excellent meals, did my laundry and any mending that was required.

I arrived at work in good time, reporting for duty, where the foreman introduced me to my mate, then told me to go to the stores where I was issued with a pair of gauntlet gloves, a face mask and a pair of safety goggles.

My mate explained the job to me as follows. Every locomotive passed under the coal hopper where its tender was filled with coal and water. Then it moved on to the ash pit where the fire was dropped out through the firegrate, and on again to the turntable where it was placed in an empty stall. Our job was to go into the firebox and check it out for defects and leaks, making sure the tubeplate was clean. His job was to fix the defects and mine to clean down the tubeplate and blow the tubes if necessary.

It was essential that we worked together in case either one of us was affected by the firebox heat, just having had the fire dropped out.

We checked out the first locomotive, a big 4-6-4, found it to be in good order, so the boilermaker went to a small blackboard mounted at the end of the stall and marked 'Boiler OK' on it, then we moved on to the next locomotive, this time a 4-6-2 Pacific. We found that some stays were leaking so fetched an air hammer. I watched while he caulked them, then took his place in the firebox and I cleaned down the tubeplate making sure I did not touch the brick arch which was still very hot.

After we had finished this work and marked up the 'Boiler OK' sign on the blackboard, the firelighter took over. I was fascinated by the method used to light the fire because, instead of our way of using cloths soaked in paraffin, adding sleeper wood then finally hand picked coal thus creating a fire, a much more quick and efficient way was used.

Every Roundhouse stall had two air pipes situated close to the footplate to be used for several different purposes, namely working the air hammer, a rotating tool used for cleaning arch tubes, and the gun for cleaning the tubes. These had to be blown from the firebox end, as they were not accessible from the smoke box unless the spark arrester plates and the smoke box self cleaning cage were removed, a dirty and time consuming job.

To light the fire a machine resembling the old type tar sprayer was employed. This basically was a tank of paraffin on wheels with a T-shaped spray connected to it by a long flexible hose pipe and having another flexible hose attached to the rear of the tank. A second pipe was connected to the spray but bypassed the tank, so that when both pipes were coupled to the air supply the tank was pressurised to force out the paraffin whilst air was mixed with it to form an effective flame thrower.

The firelighter covered the grate area with a layer of coal, placed some lighted paper or cloth on top, turned on the sprayer which ignited then controlled the mixture to produce a fierce flame, running this over the coal which very quickly turned into a good fire covering the whole of the grate area. The locomotive was moved under its own steam back on to the turntable in order of its next duty, then moved on to the departure track. This movement was done by the Hostler or Shed Engineman as we call him.

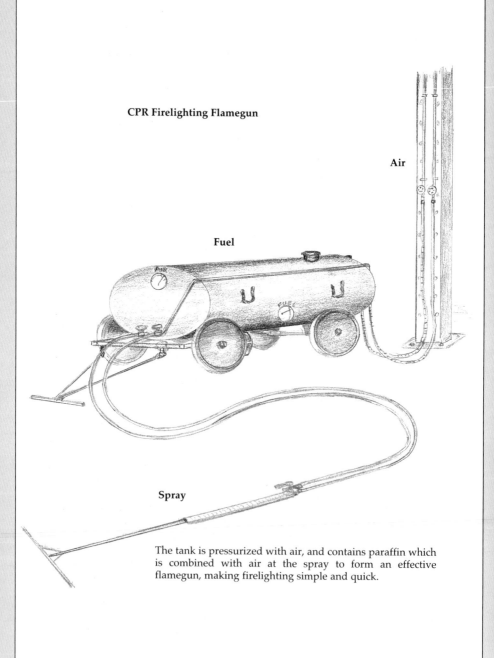

CPR Firelighting Flamegun

Air

Fuel

Spray

The tank is pressurized with air, and contains paraffin which is combined with air at the spray to form an effective flamegun, making firelighting simple and quick.

When we stopped for a break we went to the canteen, which was run by a blind man, as efficiently as anyone could have done. In fact, he even knew the exact value of the note you gave him although Canadian bank notes are all the same size. During our meal I told my mate, 'I want a fireman's job and the Employment Office have told me I can transfer to that position when there is a vacancy'. To which he replied, 'They are putting you on boy, we have men here who have been waiting for three years and they are in the right grade but you are not so your chances are nix!'

Very disappointed I decided to go to the CPR employment office on completion of duty and have it out with them.

Meanwhile it was back to work but this time we had a 'cold job' to do on a locomotive that had just been washed out, so first we went into the firebox and dismantled the brick arch, throwing the old bricks out into the cab. In Canadian locomotives the brick arch was supported on tubes running from the front of the firebox to a point at the back above the firehole door, with the number of tubes varying according to the size of the firebox. The firebricks were in various sizes and shapes, coded by letter and number e.g A1, B3, C2 etc., designed to fit securely between the arch tubes. My job was to fetch them from the stockpile whilst the boilermaker busied himself caulking some stays.

On my return he told me the tubes needed a clean, so I connected the gun to the air supply, then when he had finished in the firebox I took his place, taking the gun with me and started to blow the tubes. After the first few I found one that was blocked, so, of course, as soon as I turned on the air at 100 lb. per square inch, instead of going through the tube it came straight back bringing with it stinging ash before I could duck out of the way, but I did not get caught again and made sure that I kept out of the line of fire.

When I had finished the tubes, we rebuilt the brick arch, a task that was completed in a short space of time. My mate instructed me in the order of placement (so that I could do it on my own in future) as he handed the bricks in to me, this being the accepted way of doing it.

With the firebox work completed, our next job was to clean the inside of the arch tube. This was done by removing caps on the boiler back and inserting a tool with three toothed wheels on the end, again operated by air. When the air was turned on and the wheels started to revolve it was lowered down the tube until the front end was reached. This was repeated until they were all done, then the caps were replaced and tightened.

The next job was to water test the boiler, which was accomplished by connecting a pressurized water hose to a special fitting on the injector overflow pipe then turning on the water until the steam gauge registerd 100 lb. per square inch. The boiler was checked out for leaks, as water will seep out where even steam cannot escape. Finding no leaks we released the water pressure then disconnected the hose, finally marking up the inevitable blackboard with 'Boiler OK'.

At 9.0 am I was waiting for the door to open at the Canadian Pacific employment office which was situated in the main hall of Toronto's large Union station. Upon being admitted I asked for an explanation as to why I was misinformed about the possibility of a transfer to a fireman's job. The attitude of the clerical officer was that I should consider myself lucky to have a job.

I left the office feeling very low in spirit, spotting as I did so the Canadian National employment office immediately opposite, so I went straight there enquiring and asked whether there were any vacancies for firemen. The answer was 'yes' and the clerk explained the procedure I had to follow. 'First of all you have to fill out an application for employment, then you have to sign a declaration to purchase a Railway watch. This will cost around $100 but do not let that worry you as you can get it on credit at the appointed suppliers'.

When I had completed the forms, he took them and ushered me into a small room explaining, 'Your next task is to answer this set of questions, but you have a time limit. I will set this clock, then when the alarm sounds bring them straight to me and do not finish the question you are on'. I felt rather apprehensive when he added, 'There's 50 questions and you are allowed 12 minutes to complete them'. He left me to the task which I did with gusto, but when the alarm went I had not finished the questions.

To my relief the clerk told me that no one ever completed the questions adding, 'We are more than satisfied if you have done 25'. I explained 'I have finished 38'. He seemed surprised at that and told me that I had done very well! After checking them he told me that my answers were they are all correct and for that I was truly thankful.

Thinking that was all I felt relaxed, then nonplussed when he handed me several more sets of questions which he told me that there was no time limit for completion.

I found I had been given papers on: Maths, Spelling, History, Geography, General Knowledge and Mechanical Aptitude, all of which I completed but it took me five hours in all for the test. By this time I was feeling very tired having worked all night. I handed the papers back to him for checking and felt pleased with my efforts when he said, 'You have got the job; now if you would like to go along to the Medical Centre they will test your eyes, but it will be two weeks before you can see the doctor as he is fully booked until then'.

I explained that I had had no sleep for 30 hours and, in fact, had a job to keep my eyes open, so an appointment was made for me the following morning at 9.00 am for an eye test and on 25th June with the Doctor.

I passed the eye test and the physical examination without difficulty. I was given the certificate and told to report to the Master Mechanic at the CNR Roundhouse at Spadina Avenue for further instructions. He asked a few questions about previous experience, declined offered references, saying, 'We don't need them, we will soon find out if you are OK!' Then he directed me to a coach in the marshalling yard for interview by the Rules Inspector after which I was to report back to the roster clerk. The latter would give me a Student Fireman's pass to go out on a steam locomotive, to be repeated until an Engineer signed me off as fit to do the job.

The Rules Inspector was an elderly man who, after a few questions, gave me a Rule Book, a Toronto Terminals Railway timetable, a book of safety rules and a switch key, for which I signed. He then gave me a small folder with questions on rules, for the answers to which you had to look up the Rule in the Rule Book, thus proving you had, at least, read the rule.

He read through my answers then, nodding approval, he asked 'Well what do you think of our Rules?'. Being honest I replied, 'They do not seem safe to me. There are instances when you can pass a signal at danger, such as Stop and Proceed signals, also Grade signals. Its true you have to stop but you are allowed to proceed at the first type, but at the second type, the Grade signal, if you have more than 50 per cent of a full load, you can, providing you reduce speed, pass it without stopping. That is something I have not been used to'.

He assured me that if you carried out those rules to the letter that they were safe so, satisfied, I thanked him and made my way back to see the roster clerk, who gave me a Student Fireman's pass, writing down the number of an 0-8-0 tender loco which was soon to leave the Roundhouse to do some switching or shunting at a nearby yard.

The driver, or should I say engineer, was near to retirement but the fireman had only six years service in whilst, at that time, I was a Passed Fireman, fully qualified to drive steam locomotives with 13 years service. I acquainted them with these facts to which the Fireman said, 'You have twice the service in on steam as I have, how can I teach you anything?', so in reply I asked that he showed me the injectors and how they worked, also the firehole door controls, bell controls, as well as any others I had to operate. This he willingly did, then seeing that I fully understood them said to the engineer, 'This man, obviously, knows more about the job than I do, is there any point in him staying here?'. The engineer seemed reluctant to let me go, so I stayed on for two hours doing the firing, after which time he handed me back the Student Pass saying, 'Don't take any notice of what I have written on it, but I am responsible for you!'

Glancing at it I read 'a little more experience required' so back to the office I went to make arrangements for further 'education'.

The next day I went out on another 0-8-0 tender loco which had a tractive effort of around 50,000 lb., way above that of a 'Merchant Navy', and the job we were on was transferring freight from one yard to another. The engineer this time was much younger and on being informed of my previous record said, 'We have to work a heavy freight to a yard five miles away, so if you do the firing and make her steam OK, then I will sign you off as fit to do the job'.

We had a load of 75 freight cars, the shortest of which was 40 ft long, so the total length was in excess of ¾ of a mile, with a weight of over 3,000 tons. The locomotive was fitted with a firehole door exactly like a 'West Country's', made by Ajax, with the same controls but worked by air instead of steam which I found to be an advantage having a more positive action and less prone to failure. The fireman offered me his gloves which I declined because I had never worn any before. He said, 'I think you will need them, but see how you make out first'.

The firebox of this locomotive was large compared to ours and the coal was small nuts, ideally suited to locomotives fitted with automatic stokers. Care had to be taken not to overload the fire because this gave off volumes of smoke which was taboo and was very easy to do with this coal, hence the need for the old method of 'little and often'.

The engineer got the 'highball' which is the right away signal, so with a blast on the beautiful sounding chime whistle, he eased open the throttle taking up the slack of the automatic couplers, then with the whole train on the move he gave a good tug at it, until it was almost fully opened. This produced a roar of exhaust far louder than any of our locomotives make, with a column of smoke and steam from the smokestack as straight as a ramrod.

He notched up the valve gear to around 40 per cent, then I started to shovel coal into the firebox, applying pressure to the door treadle in the middle of the swing. By the natural transference of weight from one foot to the other, with the door hissing open to accept the coal, I repeated this with an easy rhythm but, after a few good shovelfuls, the back of my left hand was stinging with the heat. I turned to the fireman saying, 'You were right about the gloves, my hand is as hot as hell', so with a wry smile he handed me his which I readily accepted with grateful thanks.

With the steam gauge moving towards the red line, I put on the injector cutting it fairly fine, then carried on firing, gratified to see the steam was still on the make. I eased open the door with the manual lever which brought a remark from the engineer, 'We don't usually leave the firehole door open!' so I said, 'I am doing it to prevent her from blowing off'. He grinned as he said, 'OK boy, do it your way'.

Opening the door had brought quite a reduction in the amount of smoke issuing from the smokestack, chimney that is, and kept the steam pressure nicely under control which was my aim because, in common with most Canadian locomotives this engine was not fitted with dampers.

Nearing a highway crossing, the engineer sounded the whistle, giving the appropriate code, 2 long, 1 short and 1 long, also opening the valve for the bell which was air operated with a piston moving inside a fixed bell, because the law calls for its use. We were now nearing our destination so the engineer eased the throttle, then closed it, dropping the lever down into full gear, then started to apply the Westinghouse brake, gently bringing the speed down as we went through the switch, or points to us, and he finally brought the train gently to a halt at the end of the reception road.

I had fully opened the firehole door as we entered the yard and opened the water feed wider, thus slightly reducing the steam pressure to prevent making unnecessary noise. The yard man cut off the engine and we picked up another train, waiting for our train crew, which consisted of a freight conductor and two brakemen. When all was ready we got the 'highball', then with a light load set off on a line that ran completely around Toronto, appropriately called the Belt Line. This serviced all kinds of factories and warehouses, including a timber yard or lumber yard as they call it, where we had to set off two loaded flat cars piled high with timber.

As we set back into the yard the grab iron, or handrail, caught a length of timber that was, unfortunately, being stacked too close to the track and sent the whole stack crashing down, with the workmen just jumping clear in time. No blame was attached to us, and apart from the work that had to be done all over again, no one was hurt I am glad to say.

At this point the engineer said, 'Give me your student papers and I will sign you off as OK so that you can start right away as a fireman. You handled the job well and I can see you know what to do'.

I felt happy to know that now I could do the job that I really wanted. I watched as he wrote 'NO FURTHER EXPERIENCE NECESSARY' in large capital letters, signing it with a flourish then handing it to me, wishing me, 'Good Luck Stan, keep your nose clean', then adding, 'You can catch a streetcar from here that will take you straight back to the Roundhouse'. Thanking them both I took leave of them and made my way back to the depot.

The clerk took the papers from me remarking that only two days as a student, must be some kind of a record. He told me that there was just one other thing you have to do and that is to go out on a diesel switcher to get passed out on that. Handing me a student's pass he continued, 'You will see No. 8451 out in the coach yard, go take a look at that'.

I found No. 8451 which was an Alco 1000 hp diesel electric switcher, or shunter, that had been introduced to take over switching duties from the 0-8-0 and 0-6-0 tender steam locomotives that had served the CNR so well for many years. These locomotives were destined to finish out their remaining life on short haul transfer freight work.

Climbing up into the cab I was greeted by the engineer, dressed from head to toe in light fawn coloured cap, shirt and trousers. Handing him the Student's Pass I explained, 'They have sent me out to learn the diesel so that I can start work as a Fireman'. Noting my accent he asked where I came from. On telling him he extended his hand in friendship saying, 'Put it there Stan, I came from London 40 years ago'; not that I would have guessed it because he had a strong Canadian accent.

I put him in the picture about my previous experience on steam and straight away he said, 'I'll sign your paper, with your years on steam you will do fine'. Whereupon I said, 'I don't know anything about diesels'. He laughed saying, 'Thats OK, neither do I'.

I thought I had better know something about them as I did not want to appear to be a complete novice, so I asked him to tell me my duties on them and give me a quick rundown as well. This he did, proving that he knew a lot more than he had suggested.

All diesels at that time had an engineer and a fireman, not that there was much for the fireman to do, but they were not fitted with a Driver's Safety Device, hence the two men. I stayed chatting to them both for an hour then walked back to the Roundhouse, handing in my form at the office, only to be asked, 'When can you start work?'

I explained that I was working for the CPR as a boilermaker's helper and that I would have to give them notice, but the clerk said, 'You are employed on a daily basis, so you can hand in your notice when you start work tonight, then you will be able to finish your spell with them in the morning'. I found this to be correct; in fact, I was given a form to take to the Canadian Pacific Express office where I was paid in full for three weeks' work.

Whilst I was doing all that was necessary to gain employment as a fireman I did not receive any payment for it, hence it had been necessary to keep my job on the CPR for financial reasons but I found it very tiring because I had very little time for sleep. During this three week period I had on occasion worked with a boilermaker who was a full blooded Red Indian of the Blackfoot tribe and although his features were true to this mongoloid race his appearance certainly was not. He wore striped bib and brace overalls, a cloth cap and was never seen without a big fat cigar in the corner of his mouth; very reminiscent of the comedy film star Ned Sparks, with the same deadpan expression.

Some things always stick in my mind and I can still picture the large workshop at the CPR Roundhouse with its modern tools and machinery so contrasting to the fitters' shop at Bournemouth which had a lathe over 100 years old, a shaping machine, a vice, a grinding wheel plus a motley assortment of hand tools.

Canadian locomotives were very easy to service, with all the piping readily accessible on the outside running along the boiler, giving rise to the expression 'a plumber's nightmare'. The firelighting process mentioned earlier was excellent, also it was possible to have an air powered blower even if the engine was out of steam. This was done by removing a plug at a point where the external blower pipe entered the side of the smokebox and connecting an overhead air supply to it by means of a flexible pipe. To raise steam was a simple and quick operation using both these features because the fire could be lit in minutes, whilst the blower could be used immediately.

Having terminated my CPR job I was now free to start my new job as a CNR fireman. I was relieved when the roster clerk said, 'You can start work at 7.00 am Wednesday morning, that will give you a night in bed so that you will feel fit for it. You will be booked on a regular duty known as the Jefferson Avenue job, which is a switching turn servicing the factories within the Belt line during the day and doing yard work at night. You will have three shifts, 7.00 am, 3.00 pm and 11.00 pm, that, of course, is Railway Time which is the same all the year round, but as we are now into Summer time that will make it 8.00 am, 4.00 pm and midnight city time'.

He went on to explain that I did not have to report to the Depot, but to go straight to the yard at Spadina Avenue and join the locomotive there. He gave me my employee's number, 876210 and told me that the engineer on the early shift was always Ed Broomer which puzzled me because no one on British Railways kept a job all the time, with the possible exception of a light duty man doing permanent night shed engineman's duties. Leaving the office I made my way over to the yard, just to make sure how to get there and made enquiries of the yard supervisor as to where to find the engine.

I arrived in good time, found the Alco 1000 hp switcher No. 8457 without difficulty, and introduced myself to the engineer, Ed Broomer. I explained that I was not entirely a newcomer and was passed for driving on British Railways, but was new to Canadian Railways so, obviously had a lot to learn.

Ed explained our duties for the day and also cleared up the 'mystery' of being on one turn all the time. Each year the roster was put out, then the engineer who was the senior man picked out the turn of duty he wanted, which would probably be a day job around 8.00 am involving mileage payment if he was fit, then engineer No. 2 had his pick and so on until all of the jobs were covered. The day jobs were mostly covered by older men, the afternoon jobs by the middle aged, whilst the nights were left to the younger men.

This struck me as being fine for the senior men, but I wondered what sort of jobs the junior men would be stuck with. Ed explained that an engineer could elect to go into the spare link taking any job that came along, covering holidays, sickness and specials. By doing so he had to be prepared to sign on at a different time every day, doing long hours during the summer when there was lots of extra work around and during the winter face the prospect of being booked off without pay, if there was insufficient work to go round.

We were soon joined by the yard men assigned to this duty, that is to say the foreman and two yardmen or head shunter and two shunters as we would call them. They also had the same system of promotion and all three were in their sixties with over 100 years service between them so they were no novices.

They greeted the engineer with a, 'Hi Ed', then enquiring my name added, 'Hi, Stan, glad to know you', which at once put me at ease.

We spent a busy morning 'spotting' freight cars at various factories and pulling out the ones ready for shipment. Then, around noon we stopped outside a large mill where all kinds of paper products were made such as large rolls of wrapping paper, several feet in diameter, cardboard packing cases, in fact, almost everything that is made of woodpulp.

We went into the large spotlessly clean canteen where we had coffee and doughnuts, spending a very interesting half hour listening to the foreman who had just returned from a fishing holiday on the Texas coast. He had a delightful way of relating his adventures that had us in stitches as it was full of good natured humour.

The rest of the day continued as before, then we took the collected cars back down to the yard at Spadina Avenue where we detached them and waited for relief. When the new crew arrived we exchanged pleasantries. As I was about to leave the fireman said, 'Don't forget that you have to come back to relieve me at midnight will you?'

Thunderstruck I said, 'But I have done today's work!' Then he explained that Wednesday was changeover day for the firemen and that I had to come back again to do the night duty.

Quite taken aback I said, 'Well if that is the way it works OK, I will relieve you as booked', but I hated the idea of it as I had never liked working nights. As I only had eight hours off duty, sleep was out of the question and I had managed to get a good night's rest on Tuesday, so I just took it easy.

I relieved the fireman on time then introduced myself to the engineer to be greeted with the query, 'Where's my mate?' I explained that this was now my job having started that morning on the day shift.

The engineer said that he had been to a wedding and had not worried about sleep as his mate had said that he would do the switching that night.

When I explained that, although it was my first day I had lots of experience, he was greatly relieved and said, 'If you can drive a steamer you can drive one of these!' I had to explain that I had never worked at night switching in Canada, therefore, I didn't know the hand lamp signals which are all given with a white light, using a lamp which closely resembles a storm lantern but with a shorter glass and having the well packed with wadding to prevent it going out if waved violently or inverted.

On starting work he said, 'Come over and stand behind me, then I will

explain the yardman's tips as he gives them; you will soon learn what they are'.
In about 10 minutes I had a full understanding of them and called them out
so that the engineer was in no doubt about it. He got out of his bucket type seat
saying, 'Well there you are, there's the brake, there's the reverse, there's the
throttle and there's the headlight dip switch. Call me if you want me'.

He went over to the fireman's side seat which was a large box about 3 ft 6 in.
long by 1 ft 8 in. wide nicely padded with foam. He placed two wooden framed
storm window panels at one end, resting them on the back window sill, which
made a reasonable bed, then using his coat for a pillow laid down and slept
soundly for six hours!

The switching presented me with no problems as I found the diesel a joy to
handle, very responsive with lots of power and a brake that kept one fully in
control even with a long string of freight cars.

During the time the engineer was asleep we stopped for a meal break, and I
joined the yard men who were around my age; the foreman being a Pole, the
second an Italian and the third a Canadian. With me being English we made a
very cosmopolitan group. The Canadian asked how long I had been driving
diesels, to which I, of course, replied that this was the first time.

Having finished our meal seated on a pile of ties (sleepers) on that beautiful
summer night, the foreman said that our next job was to take a string of cars
across to the other yard ready to go out in the morning. Climbing aboard where
the engineer was still sleeping peacefully, I picked up the cars, then with the
yard crew riding on the engine pulled up to the switch ready to cross over the
main line into the reception road of the other yard.Toronto station was as
modern as it could be, with colour light signalling, heated switches and a first
class signal box. But the first junction westward was in complete contrast
having hand pulled switches operated by a switchtender who received his
instructions over a loud speaker from the control tower, which operated the
signals but not the switches. At each switch there was a switchstand which was
a waist high frame with a lever to change the switch, the lever being padlocked
in the locked position.

To operate the switch it was necessary to unlock the padlock with a switch
key, lift the lever, turn it through 90° to throw the switch, then lower the lever
and padlock in the secure position. Rising from the switchstand was a rod to
which was fixed a lamp having four aspects, two being green the other two
being red so that when the switch was set for the main line it showed green in
each direction, but when it was reversed it showed red.

I was now faced with this red light when I was given the 'highball' by the
switchtender so I turned to the foreman for advice. He told me, 'Thats OK,
that's a switch, it is alright to go'. I opened the throttle, easing the train out
across the main line, asking at each switch, 'OK?' being assured, 'Yep, thats a
switch', but feeling very uneasy when passing that 'red' and more than relieved
when we reached the other yard. However, having passed four red lights they
lost their importance and with another one facing me I would have cheerfully
passed it but was brought sharply back to reality when the foreman told me the
next one was a signal. So with a couple of touches on the Westinghouse air
brake I brought her to a stand saying 'That put years on me! I'm not used to

'King Arthur' class 4-6-0 No. 30784 *Sir Nerovens* crosses Canute Road at No. 5 Gates to work a boat train to Waterloo, 10th September, 1955.   *E.R. Morten*

A flagman stands in the middle of Canute Road whilst BR Standard class '4MT' 2-6-0 leaves Southampton Docks with a freight train on 10th September, 1955.   *E.R. Morten*

BR Standard 2-10-0 class '9F' No. 92205 leaves Southampton with a 'Pigeon Special' for the Bournemouth line, 11th May, 1963. *Roy Panting*

Maunsell 'U' class 2-6-0 No. 31618 passes Millbrook with a down van train to Bournemouth, 8th June 1962. *Roy Panting*

Southern Region 1Co-Co1 diesel electric locomotive No. 10202 passes over the level crossing at Brockenhurst on the down 'Bournemouth Belle'.   *Ron Goult*

Maunsell 'Q' class 0-6-0 No. 30539 stands at Brockenhurst, waiting to leave with a train for Bournemouth West via the 'Old Road' through Ringwood with a 2-car push and pull set.

Real Photographs

Ex-LSWR Drummond 0-6-0 '700' 'Black Motor' class No. 30690 waits to leave Brockenhurst with a down local pick-up goods for Bournemouth.   *Ron Goult*

BR Standard class '4MT' 2-6-4T passes under the footbridge at Brockenhurst with a freight from Bournemouth. Note the electric conductor rail has been installed on the up line, whilst the insulators and chairs are in place on the down line with the rail waiting to be fitted, 30th August, 1966.   *Roy Panting*

Ex-GWR 'Hall' class 4-6-0 No. 6923 *Croxteth Hall* climbs Sway bank with the 10.17 am York-Bournemouth West, 16th May, 1964. In the distance is Lymington Junction and you can just make out the formation of the 'Old Road' to Ringwood and Broadstone (to the left) and of the Lymington branch (to the right). *Roy Panting*

'Remembrance' class 4-6-0 No. 32331 *Beattie* approaches Christchurch down platform with a Waterloo-Bournemouth train carrying duty '38' headcode, 18th July, 1953. *Ron Goult*

LMS diesel electric No. 10000 at Pokesdown station on a down Waterloo train during evaluation trials over Southern metals.   *Ron Goult*

My own engine, 'Merchant Navy' class 4-6-2 No. 35027 *Port Line* running through Pokesdown on the up 'Royal Wessex'. The best locomotive I ever worked on!   *Ron Goult*

Ex-LNER 2-6-2 class 'V2' No. 60893 on the up 'Bournemouth Belle' at Bournemouth Central, 23rd May 1953. These locomotives had been drafted in from the Eastern Region after an axle failure on a 'West Country' class locomotive at Crewkerne lead to a temporary withdrawal from service of Bulleid Pacifics. *Roy Panting*

BR Standard class '4MT' 2-6-0 No. 76014 coming off stock which it had just brought from Bournemouth West. This stock will be shunted onto a Weymouth-Waterloo train, 24th May, 1953. *Roy Panting*

'Lord Nelson' class 4-6-0 No. 30852 *Sir Walter Raleigh* passes through Bournemouth Central on its way to Bournemouth depot. *Roy Panting*

This view from the down platform at west end of Bournemouth Central station with 'S15' class 4-6-0 No. 30502 on a train of loco coal for Bournemouth depot, 14th September, 1957. The depot is just out of view to the left of the photographer. *Roy Panting*

passing red lights!'.

He assured me, 'You will soon get to know these switches' which I found to be perfectly true.

All switches around the yards were fitted with two green and two yellow lights so that when the lead track was set for the straight you had a row of green lights, but when any switch was pulled that light turned to yellow, although the levers were not padlocked but secured by a curved hook on a chain.

Should you happen to run through a wrongly set CNR switch, little damage was done but if it was a CPR switch, the mechanism was smashed up and you were on the carpet!

Canadian train crews were given 'de-merit' marks for various offences, such as being late on duty, failing to have your watch checked on time, running through switches etc., and if you accumulated 60 you were fired. Three firemen were given the sack while I was over there because, although they had not reached a count of 60, their rate of accumulation was such that by the law of averages they could not finish their time on the railway, so they were politely asked to leave.

The rule in regard to watches, which are all important in North America was as follows. Your watch must be checked at not less an interval than 20 days or more than 30 days or at any time should the variation reach 30 seconds, when it should be taken to a designated watch inspector for correction. It was also a rule that when starting a duty the train crew, which consisted of five men, had to compare watches and should the variation be more than 30 seconds it was necessary to contact Central Time Control to ascertain the correct time. This was given right down, not to the minute, but to the second, so important was it for the safe working of trains. (On a passenger train it was the engineer, fireman, passenger conductor, and two trainmen. On a freight train besides the engine crew you had a freight conductor, a head end brakeman and a rear end brakeman. On a Switching duty you had, in addition to the engine crew, a foreman and two yard men.)

A new employee was given three month's grace before having to purchase a watch, so in consequence I never did buy one, thus saving $100.

At the end of that night's work the engineer thanked me for doing the switching for him but I had to admit that I enjoyed it, even though I was feeling very tired and thankful that it was time for relief.

The following week when I was on the afternoon shift, I had more time to observe train movements and I watched in awe as a Toronto Hamilton and Buffalo Railway (TH&B) night sleeper pulled out of Toronto with 20 sleeping cars in tow, each weighing 87 tons, which was about equal to 45 of our coaches.

This train was pulled by a New York Central 'J3' class 4-6-4 which had two 28 inch cylinders assisted by a booster unit under the cab, giving it a power far in excess of any locomotive in service here. Although the engine was 100 yards away, the blast from the smokestack was so strong that it plucked at my shirt sleeve resting on the armrest of the General Motors EMD Switcher on which I was working.

The TH&B was a joint railway between the New York Central (NYC) and the Canadian Pacific with NYC supplying the motive power, but the CPR providing the coaches, although on the night sleeper the cars were a mixed bag of several different companies.

Some of the 'J3' class locomotives had NYC painted on the tender, while others were inscribed TH&B. All of them were in good condition, were a beautiful design and could not fail to impress anyone with a love of steam locomotives, such was their obvious power.

The Jefferson Avenue job proved to be very interesting, because we did a variety of work; one Sunday afternoon we were taking some boxcars across a roadway that had recently been resurfaced with tarred stones, when one boxcar became derailed because the channel for the wheels had become blocked by loose stones. Without fuss or panic the yard crew set to work with a will, unhooking the re-railer ramps from the side of the locomotive and placing them in front of the derailed truck or bogie; then giving the engineer the 'go ahead' signal, watching closely as he eased the boxcar forward to make sure that the wheels ran back on to the rails.

The whole operation took less than 10 minutes from start to finish with the re-railers placed back on to the special hooks on the side of the diesel switcher.

Steam locomotives also carried these re-railers attached to the tender underframe between the trucks or bogies and I can testify as to their efficiency as twice more during that day the same empty boxcar came off the track at precisely the same spot, but each time was put back on track just as quickly.

The foreman put a card on the car requesting a thorough examination of the truck in case it was out of alignment but it was the only empty boxcar and I believe it was not heavy enough to push the compacted stone out of the way.

The permanent way maintenance gang were informed so that the track channels could be cleared out to prevent a recurrence of the incidents.

On another occasion we had picked up some boxcars loaded with very large rolls of paper weighing several tons each, from the Hinde and Dache Paper Mill and were pushing them out towards the yard around a sharp curve close to a large warehouse owned by Loblaws Supermarkets. At that moment a large lorry of the tractor and trailer type pulled away from the loading area but failed to turn enough and mounted the track. The engineer immediately slammed on the emergency brake but the weight of the cars dragged us on and the leading boxcar struck the nearside of the tractor sending it high in the air, trapping it there with the driver looking down from a height of about 12 feet.

By sheer luck the driver was unhurt but was distraught because he had only had the job for one day and had not driven that make of lorry before so he was fearful in case he was given the sack, as it was entirely his fault. The engineer put in a report but heard no more about the incident.

During the time I was in Canada the Canadian Pacific introduced the first diesel electric-hauled trans-continental express passenger train consisting of streamlined stainless steel coaches which included Vista Dome cars and an observation car at the rear, all built by the Budd Company of America.

This train started from Montreal and went right through to Vancouver, then back again, which is a round trip of almost 6,000 miles. The locomotives were built by the Electro Motive Division of General Motors and were run in 'A' and 'B' unit formation, that is to say the leading 'A' unit had a cab at one end, the 'B' unit had no cab but was of the same power, being driven from the 'A' unit and a typical formation could be A-B-A or A-B-B-A according to the power required.

The Canadian National had recently placed into service diesel electric locomotives in A-B formation built by Fairbanks Morse for use on heavy freight trains and the load out of Toronto for these was 4,600 tons; but they were often assisted by a steam locomotive which was often a massive '4100' class 2-10-2 which had two large cylinders plus a booster unit giving them enormous power.

The '4100' class had the largest diameter boilers in the British Empire, being fitted with a feedwater heater and a Duplex automatic stoker. They could be worked hard for long periods which made them capable of pulling a load of 6,500 tons unassisted in good weather.

During bad weather there was a fixed reduction in loads, i.e if the temperature was from zero to 10 degrees below freezing the reduction in tonnage was 15 per cent and if it was 46° to 50° below freezing the reduction was 50 per cent.

Regrettably I only worked on steam locomotives on three occasions, each time on a 0-8-0 tender locomotive, which were hand fired, being built for switching duties and having large cylinders, driving small wheels resulting in high tractive effort which was easy to maintain with the large firebox provided.

Working on the diesels gave me plenty of time to study the engines that were working on the main line, as we were close to it, in a slightly elevated position and nearly all of the switching was on a slight curve on the engineer's side. This left me free to watch both CNR and CPR trains that passed us in both directions and I saw all types of locomotives: 2-8-2s, 2-10-2s, 2-8-0s, 2-8-4s, 4-6-4s, 4-6-2s and big 4-8-4s.

The design of some Canadian Pacific locomotives was very different to those of the CNR, being very smooth looking with all the piping concealed and the steam dome as well as the sand domes hidden away under casing. This gave the impression that the boilers were much larger than they really were, which coupled with their smart maroon and grey paint made them distinctive. My favourite locomotive without a doubt was the streamlined '6400' class 4-8-4s of the CNR. These locomotives were fully covered in a very smooth shroud which hid the smokestack domes, the air pumps and reservoirs, plus all the piping etc.

The tenders were of the Vanderbuilt type that were cylindrical at the rear but square at the front for the coal section. The whole locomotive was painted in two tones of green divided by a yellow stripe whilst the logo was bright red with yellow lettering. The finishing touch was the white painted hand rails and driving wheel tyres, all of which could not fail to impress anyone used to the much smaller British Railways locomotives.

Ed Broomer telephoned me at my lodge one day inviting me over to supper after we finish work the following day. I thanked him for the invitation, adding, 'That will be great Ed, I'll look forward to it'.

We finished work at 4.00 pm the next day, then set off for Ed's place which was due north, straight up Spadina Avenue, almost to the city limits, picked up his wife and made our way to Loblaws Supermarket to pick up some groceries.

It was the first time I had ever been in a supermarket and I was goggle-eyed when I saw the wide range of goods on display. It must be remembered that certain things were still on ration back home and lots of others were still not available in 1952.

Ed's wife gave me a grand meal and they were very kind to me. We had a few beers, went through lots of photographs, talking about all aspects of railways which added up to a very enjoyable evening.

Noting the time was 11.00 pm I said, 'I had better get going, I did not realize it was as late as that'. Then much to my surprise Ed said, 'That's Railway time, it is actually midnight City time, we always keep the clocks that way and don't alter them for summer time, it saves confusion about getting to work on time'. I apologised for staying so late, thanked them warmly and hurried to the street car stop in case I missed the last car home, but I need not have worried as they ran until 1.00 am.

I liked the job as a CNR fireman very much, but I did not like the prospect of years of night and afternoon shifts when I eventually became an engineer. So I decided to return home to take up my position again as a No. 1 Link fireman back on good old No. 34108; I booked my passage home on the RMS *Samaria*, which sailed on 10th September, 1952.

I have often wondered if I would have been better off staying in Canada but there is no way that I shall ever know. However, I still have pleasant memories of my days there as a CPR boilermaker's helper and a CNR fireman which fostered an interest in North American locomotives that I still have today, only now it is in the form of models of which I have a large collection which is still growing.

Switching lamp

Chapter Six

Back to Bournemouth

I went straight back into No. 1 Link along with Frank and it was hard work because during my stay in Canada I had put on 20 pounds in weight in the 14 weeks. But, in as many weeks, I was back to my normal weight of 12 stone 7 pounds and I had lost none of my enthusiasm and we still had No. 34108.

I worked with Frank for 3½ years and perhaps the most memorable day was when we were working the 'Royal Wessex' which was 10 minutes late in starting because of what is now known as 'operating difficulties'. When we left Bournemouth, Frank said, 'Let's show them what we can do and try to get that time back!' I nodded assent, knowing full well that it would mean a hard slog for me but it was a challenge which I never could resist.

The 'Royal Wessex' was a heavy 13 coach train and very sharply timed, so I knew it would take some doing and, in fact, we had only managed to get back three minutes by the time we reached Worting Junction. But after that we simply flew along passing Woking in just 17 minutes which was two minutes less than the time allowed to the REP electric units.

Easing speed slightly after Woking, we arrived at Waterloo two minutes before time, having covered 50 miles in 40 minutes dead. No. 34108 was not fitted with a speedometer so there was no real way of knowing our top speed, but we did average 75 miles per hour over the 50 miles and several passengers complimented us on our run which made it all worthwhile.

Towards the end of my time with Frank I was often taken off for driving duties which meant that I was losing 17 shillings (85p) mileage for a trip and receiving 5 pence per day extra for doing so. A classic case of an Irishman's rise!

I liked main line firing so much that when it was nearing my time to come off I tried to get the LDC agreement (local trade union agreement) - which decreed that the 12 senior passed firemen should come off main line work - reverted back to its original nine (men) but to no avail. The motion was defeated so, not long afterwards my No. 1 Link days as a fireman were over, but not forgotten.

I went back down to the 'Old Man's Link' firing to Jack Thorne, a driver off the old Somerset and Dorset line originally at Branksome shed but who, owing to the merging of our depots, was now at Bournemouth. Jack was not much older than me which made a pleasant change because up to now the age difference was great between driver and fireman, not that it mattered to me but it was something new.

As mentioned before, our work was light and varied, involving a lot of shunting work but Jack and I took turns at driving making it easier for Jack and giving me more experience at driving.

It is strange but the different areas have quite a lot of varied terms for such items as signals, fireirons, lamps to name but a few, that it could lead to confusion. We were at Hamworthy Junction one day on a freight when Jack, unfamiliar with the duty, asked me what was the plan of action. So I said, 'We reckon to nob her up now'. Jack's reaction was to say, 'I'll do that, you go and make the tea, no need to hurry', so off I went to do his bidding.

I returned about 20 minutes later expecting to find the fire made up, but instead I found Jack busy cleaning up the boiler front making it literally shine.

'What are you doing' I asked with an anxious glance at the fire which was by now fairly low. 'I am doing what you told me', Jack replied, 'I am nobbing her up'.

I had to explain. 'That's not what I meant, I meant fill up the firebox'. 'Well' said Jack, 'You should have told me to put a charge in her then I would have known what you were talking about'.

I made myself busy to build up a reasonable fire after having a good laugh over the mix up but, in future, I made sure we were both on the same wavelength when it came to information.

Jack was a fun loving man, always ready to crack a joke, always ready to help his fireman, but he was becoming disenchanted with the job, and, after being involved in an accident when I was not with him, he decided to call it a day and took a job with the Southern Electricity Board as a boiler attendant. I still see him on occasion and we talk about the 'good old days', which, on reflection, were damned good!

I stayed in the 'Old Man's Link' having two different mates, Stan Cox who was 60 plus and the other Cliff Bailey who was more my age.

Stan Cox was a betting man and loved to have a 'few bob' on the horses. He also liked to 'leg pull' and delighted in a charade when he met driver Ray Foyle in the company of others, especially traffic staff. The two of them would verbally fly at each other in what to all appearances was a heated argument often being almost held apart by concerned onlookers, but as soon as the audience was gone they would be the best of pals, highly amused by it all.

On Boxing Day, 1956 I was firing to driver Tom Alexander and we were waiting in the guards' room at Bournemouth Central to relieve the down Birkenhead train which was running late. Running foreman Bert Davis came into the room looking for a driver who knew the Waterloo line as one through train from Weymouth had been overlooked by the list clerk and, therefore, there was no one booked to relieve it.

There were three drivers in the room, but none of them knew the road so I said to Bert 'I know the road, but I am firing along with Tom'. 'Pick up your bag' said Bert, 'Take Larry Owen with you as fireman, its due in now, so get on over to save any delay'.

Dorchester driver Dodge brought the train of 12 coaches in with 'West Country' class No. 34043 and she was well back for steam and water, 140 lb. and 2 inches of water to be precise.

We pulled the water crane round and filled up the tender whilst Larry made every effort to bring her over but she was slow to respond and when it was time for us to leave we only had 200 lb. of steam and just above half a glass of water.

I took her away briskly then shut off steam at Boscombe, allowing her to coast down hill to Christchurch thus gaining more steam for the pull up through Hinton Admiral. I made use of every section of downhill track to try to better our position but it was obvious that the fire was in a very dirty condition and despite Larry's efforts with the rocking grate it was certainly going to be a hard struggle to make ends meet!

Our first booked stop was Southampton and we were held up at the home signal, so I instructed Larry to fill the boiler up into the top nut of the water gauge. With the signal cleared we pulled into the station and on stopping put the water pipe in to refill the tender. Whilst Larry was holding the pipe in I gave the fire a good lift up with the dart but this had little effect.

When it was time to leave we had 250 lb. of steam and a full glass of water, but as soon as we pulled away the steam pressure dropped back and when I shut off because the distant signal for Swathling was at caution, we were back to 140 lb. and had not put the injector on up until then.

As we were non stop to Waterloo, our chances of getting there in one go without the necessity to stop for a 'blow up' seemed impossible. The haul up the incline to the top of the bank at Litchfield may not be steep but, it is an awfully long way when you are as low in steam as we were.

It was, indeed, fortunate that we were following another train and we had several signal checks allowing us to gain a little here and there, so enabling us to keep going. No. 34043 was a strong locomotive and a free runner and we turned the top with 120 lb. of steam and only half an inch of water showing in the glass. So I thought it best to stop for a 'blow up' at Basingstoke. I gave her a reasonable amount of regulator to gain speed then shut off to coast into Basingstoke, but at the flyover at Worting the water was so low I decided not to apply the brake in case we damaged the boiler. We ran almost to Hook before I opened out again during which time we gained two inches of water but were still back on 120 lb. of steam.

Three times between Hook and Woking we were back as low as 90 lb. of steam and at that point the vacuum brake started to flicker so it called for an immediate closing of the regulator. To the credit of No. 34043, it must be said that in similar words to Winston Churchill, 'Never before in the history of railway travel, has so much distance been covered with so little'. I had only given her steam at strategic points and we eventually rolled into Waterloo with a loss of only seven minutes, which was down to us. Larry had worked like a galley slave to get steam but, when we stopped at Waterloo the clinker and ash was touching the brick arch at the front of the firebox and almost up to the rim of the door at the back end. We had relief and I told the Nine Elms driver of our plight; when I saw him two days later he said, 'How the hell you managed to make it I don't know, we only just made it going light to Nine Elms!'

We made the return journey on the cushions and we were both glad that we did not have to work back, so exhausting had it been!

It is true to say that it is the adversities that one remembers so well, whereas the best of trips are forgotten in the mists of time.

I did a lot of driving during this period and I was finally promoted to driver on 25th March, 1957, which put me permanently on the other side of the footplate.

BR 87257

FOOTPLATE
CREDIT
ADVICE

BRITISH RAILWAYS

MOTIVE POWER DEPARTMENT,

WATERLOO

.... 29th March, ... 19 57.

Will you please note that you will be .... appointed ....

from .. Psd. Fireman .... to .... Driver

with effect as from .... 25th March, ... 19 57.

For the purpose of your next firing/driving turn you will be credited with ....

....

.... T. E. CHRIMES/fs .... Signature

To ..... Psd. Fireman W.S.Symes,

BOURNEMOUTH CTL.

Chapter Seven

My Driving Days

On my promotion, I was placed into a new Link consisting of three pairs of men, the other two drivers being Bill Hayward and Peter Smith, but this was later reduced to two pairs.

My first fireman was Bill Curr and our two turns were as follows. On the early turn we signed on at 4.45 am then relieved a parcel and fish train working it forward to Parkstone then Poole where the train terminated.

We then banked up the Salisbury Goods if required to Branksome, turning the locomotive, usually a 'U' class, via the triangle of the Gas Works Junction and Bournemouth West Junction, running light to Hamworthy Junction where, after a break for breakfast, we did any shunting that was required.

After taking water we worked a freight train down the branch line to Hamworthy Goods, where we had relief at 12 noon, then after walking to Poole station we caught a train back to Bournemouth, signing off at 12.50 pm.

The late turn signed on at 12.40 pm, then we went passenger to Corfe Castle to relieve Swanage men on a freight which was standing in the yard.

We had to reverse the train by first setting the guard's brake van back on to a stopblock, then placing the empties out in the station finally picking up the van, placing it on to the train then running round. We worked the train up to Furzebrook clay sidings where we placed the empty wagons in position for loading, then picked up the loaded ones, backed them on to the van, then on to Wareham for more shunting, finally taking all the wagons for forwarding on to Hamworthy Junction.

After we arrived in the yard there we changed over with the crew of a 'B4' locomotive, taking it light to Poole for a trip down on to the Quay, taking oil, timber and grain to the ships or storage silos by the waterside. We would then shunt the wagons out, going back to Poole with coal, fish and a variety of goods that had come in by sea.

We often had long trains to bring out, often being overloaded but we did not refuse any load as we would have to make a second trip, thus making us late home.

It was often a struggle for the 'B4' over tight curves and track sometimes smothered in oil from passing lorries, but we always managed to make it back without having to split the train. When back at Poole we took the train over to the yard then at 8.30 pm went back light to Bournemouth shed which we did as quickly as possible so that Bill could catch a train to Hamworthy where he lived. Bill's train left at 8.44 pm so we could not afford to hang about but never once did he miss it, although at times it was a close run thing.

On Saturdays on this turn we got back to Hamworthy earlier, so we treated ourselves to a cooked tea of pork pie and baked beans, taking it in turns to provide and cook the goodies.

Bill was a good fireman and our days passed without incident except on one occasion when things went radically wrong. We left Corfe Castle with the usual load of empties, but this day we had a 20 ton wagon of coal next to the engine which was a '700' class Black Motor No. 695. On arrival at Furzebrook Sidings the guard, Ron Legge, uncoupled the brake van, walked forward and uncoupled the empties leaving us with the coal. He said, 'Stan, we want to place the coal in the dock, then pick up the empties, back into the dock picking up the loaded then out again on to the van. We will then place the coal and the empties back in the dock, that way the coal will be at the rear where they want it. Alright to pull up'.

We pulled forward, then Ron stopped me and uncoupled the coal, 'Give the coal a tap Stan', he said, so I gave the wagon a good tap as it was uphill into the dock, but as I did so I noticed that the empties were running down towards us. Ron endeavoured to stop the coal but to no avail and it collided with the empties completely derailing the leading wagon, throwing it out towards the branch line. The pointsman travelling with us ran round to the ground frame, phoning Corfe Castle signalman to stop the up train but it had already left, so both he and Ron ran down the track with red flag and detonators to stop the oncoming train.

They managed to stop the train, then rode forward with it in the hope that it would squeeze by the obstruction. The engine, an 'M7', passed by all right but the brake van at the rear was fitted with wide vision windows on each side and these simply would not clear, so there was no alternative but for the train to return to Corfe Castle and for the passengers to be sent from there by taxi to Wareham.

Having seen that the 'M7' got past, I suggested to the station master from Corfe, who was now on the scene, that it was possible for me to pass around the derailed wagon with No. 695, which was no wider than the 'M7', and come in the other end of the siding. I reasoned that if I gave the empties a good tug it was possible to slew the de-railed wagon hard against the rail, thus clearing the branch line, making it possible for passenger trains to run over it. He said, 'Alright Driver, lets have a go at it!'

The move was a complete success and the branch line service was re-instated with a speed restriction past the derailment.

The station master must have informed the divisional manager about my action because I received a commendation from Mr Townroe the district motive power superintendent, thanking me for my action and informing me that it would be recorded on my service record.

After about two years, I moved up into the preparation and disposal Link which was hard work for both driver and fireman. The work was hard and dirty, but there was plenty of opportunity to make extra money especially at weekends by 'disposing' of locomotives.

This is cleaning out the smokebox, cleaning the fire by removing the clinker in the firebox which, in some classes, involved using a clinker shovel 11 ft 6 in. long, an awkward and difficult task to a young fireman, then raking out the ashpan underneath the locomotive. The fireman did these tasks whilst the driver examined the engine for defects, such as steam blows, leaks, worn or missing parts, hose pipes split or frayed, brakes in need of adjusting or new brake blocks and burnt firebars, to name but a few.

S. C. TOWNROE, A.M.I.Mech.E.,
District Motive Power Supt.

BRITISH
TRANSPORT
COMMISSION

B.R. 1/9

SOUTHERN REGION   BRITISH RAILWAYS

My Ref: ER.18890

Motive Power Department,
Campbell Road,
EASTLEIGH.

11th July, 1960.

Driver W.S.R.Symes,
Motive Power Depot.
BOURNEMOUTH

Dear Sir,

    It has come to my notice that
when a wagon was derailed at
Furzebrook Sidings on May 30th,1960,
you exercised your initiative in
pulling the derailed wagon clear of
the running lines.

    Your action is appreciated
by me and I propose to enter a
Commendation on your Staff Record
for your initiative.

Yours faithfully,

Some firemen did object to this extra work but if the driver helped out then both could increase their earnings considerably. I was very fit and rather enjoyed cleaning fires because years of experience had taught me to make light work of it, using a few tricks of the trade. But it was none the less hot and dirty work, and during the summer months the temperature in the cab could be in excess of 100°F.

During preparation duties it was the driver's job to lubricate the engine, test the brake, make sure there was a full set of tools, detonators, red flags, lamps, sufficient coal and a full tank of water. He also made certain that there were spare gauge glasses, rings, string asbestos, worsted and wire for trimmings, and enough oil to last for the day.

It was the driver's duty to supervise the fireman's work and to teach him the art of firing. Also to make sure that it was all done in a safe and proper manner. Some of these youngsters were quick to learn, some were slower but willing to learn but a few objected to being told anything and in consequence were the ones most likely to cause you anxious moments. In a job that could not be successful without close teamwork, the driver had to be certain he could rely on his mate and I was very careful to try to be helpful without being too critical, thus sowing the seeds of a good working relationship.

I had several different firemen, but only had one, who shall be nameless, who just would not be told or helped so, in consequence, he caused me more problems than all the rest put together. Fortunately, I did not have him for long and I must confess I was not sorry to see him go!

My next fireman was Colin (Chalky) White, who was a bit of a rebel but we got on fairly well together and are firm friends to this day. He hated overtime but then he was young and had no responsibilities, so who could blame him!

Having learned well from Frank Carter, I never worked a locomotive any heavier than was absolutely necessary and I think Colin soon realised this. In consequence I believe he gained a certain amount of respect for me and our partnership benefited from this. We worked together for several months in a friendly mood without any working problems.

Moving up into the senior goods link, I had my next mate for only a short while, but he was a good fireman who spared no effort to make sure that everything was in apple pie order. We always had plenty of steam and the footplate was always kept in spotless condition. Such a man was Barry Sullivan who delights in the nickname of 'Basil Brush' because of his constant use of one. He would endeavour to fire in such a manner as to put a white coating on the chimney and the protection ring of the firehole door, a sure sign that the fire was at its best. He had a free and easy way and was a delight to have as a mate. No sooner had we got to know each other than it was his turn for promotion but over the years Barry has been very popular with all of his workmates, still the same 'cheerful chappie!'

I always tried to make the job as easy as I could for my mates but, at times, things happen that would try the patience of a saint. As in all jobs there is always the one that right from the start you know that will never make the grade.

One such youngster, 'Yo Yo' Smith, so named because of his skill with that toy, was booked with me on a turn to Lymington Town to work a school train. We coupled on to another locomotive in the depot, the fireman of the other loco making the attachment, then ran light together as far as Christchurch. On arrival there I said to 'Yo Yo', 'Go and uncouple mate, take your tail lamp with you!' So off he went, placing the lamp on the platform as he went in between the locomotives and uncoupled.

I watched him do it making sure he hung up the coupling and replaced the vacuum pipes on their dummies. I then walked back to the cab with him on my heels. I glanced back and saw that our tail lamp was still sitting on the platform, so I said, 'You didn't put the tail lamp on!' His quick reply was 'You didn't tell me to put it on mate!' Biting my tongue I said, 'True, but that was really the idea of taking it, so back you go and put it on!'

We went on to Lymington and worked the school train to Brockenhurst, then after doing some freight shunting we set back on to a short train of cement and were told we would not be required for about an hour. We still had our lamps on so I told 'Yo Yo', 'Take a disc board with you, place it half way up on the right side smokebox lamp bracket, then bring in your lamps and fill and clean them, then put them away in the locker!'

Taking a disc board with him he went round to the front of the locomotive, a Standard class '4' No. 76026, while I settled down to read the *Model Railroader* magazine I had in my bag. A steady knocking sound came from the front of the engine, continuing for several minutes until no longer able to contain my curiosity I went round to find out the cause.

On these engines the smokebox handrail was close to the lamp bracket and although a lamp would go on, a disc board would not unless you reversed it.

'Yo Yo' was stood there repeatedly banging the handrail in an effort to push it back far enough to get the disc board on but, as it was at least 1¼ inches in diameter, it could not possibly move. Exasperated, I shouted, 'Turn the disc board upside down mate, then hang it on, put your lamps out, then bring them back to the footplate'. I turned my back and as I started to walk away a lamp whistled by my ear and there was a thump behind me. I wheeled round to see 'Yo Yo' lying flat on his back but it was obvious that he was not hurt. I enquired, 'What made you jump off the framings backwards?' He was slightly winded but he replied, 'I didn't jump off backwards mate, I jumped off but the middle lamp bracket went up inside my overall jacket!'

The lamp bracket had arrested his fall, turned him over and ripped his overall buttons off in the process, causing the lamp to fly through the air narrowly missing me! For one moment I thought he had thrown it at me! Making certain he was unhurt, I turned away, finding it difficult to keep a straight face.

'Yo Yo' did not stay on the job for long, which was a blessing for us that did. Where he went no one knows. Fortunately lads like him were few and far between.

I had two more good mates, one was Keith Sloper, the other Mike Goode, who sadly died at a very early age. Keith later moved to Swanage taking a vacancy there as fireman, but he later left the job for reasons best known to himself.

'Clive' Brooker was my next fireman and he joined me late in 1962 and one incident that I shall never forget took place on the night of the 1962-63 blizzard. We were booked on duty at 1.25 am and at 9.00 pm the previous night it was obvious that I would be unable to ride my moped to work as the snow was already about a foot deep. I told my wife that I would catch a bus at 10.00 p.m to be sure of getting to work as I lived three miles from the station. So I set off on foot to walk to the bus stop. A bus appeared after 45 minutes but, only took me as far as the main road, the driver deciding that conditions were too bad to continue, not that I blamed him.

I started to walk the remaining two miles in the swirling snow, then a car came along, so I gave him the sign of a hitch hiker and much to my surprise he stopped with a cheery, 'Hop in mate, where are you off to in this lot?' I explained that I had to get to the station to work the down mail train. It was further than he had to go but he took me most of the way for which I was most grateful. So thanking him, I bade him goodnight then walked the rest of the way to the depot. I was well wrapped up but the snow had penetrated everywhere so I dried out after making myself a badly needed cup of tea. It was now after midnight and 'Clive' arrived in time to share the tea I had made.

By the time we were ready to leave with the Mail train, there was about two feet of level snow, but owing to its light texture the locomotive No. 34044 ploughed through it with ease. However, the front window soon became impossible to see through, so I had to lean out over the side. This locomotive had the older narrow cab and the Bissel truck axle box beneath the footplate sent up a stream of snow straight into my face. Luckily I had my dust goggles with me and this made it possible for me to see through the blinding snow.

Finding the signals was difficult and we were now running into deeper snow, then we were halted by the signal at Worgret Junction. We saw the signalman making his way towards us through drifts that were up to his chin and when he got to us he called up, 'I can't pull the signal off, but you have got the road alright, so pass it at danger. From the box I can see that the snow in the cutting is deep in drifts so take it easy'.

We pulled away past the signal box and ran into a drift so deep that snow came in through the roof vent, which is about 13 feet above the rail height, but we were quickly through it only to find that now the level of snow was up to the tops of the level crossing gates, with the only evidence of their position being a red lamp, seemingly resting on the snow.

By now our speed was down to a steady 40 miles per hour and no amount of coaxing would increase it, so I settled for that knowing it could have been far worse.

We ran into Dorchester station where a porter was pushing through snow, making his way to the phone at the signal, which was at danger. He literally dived into the snow, almost disappearing from view, then emerged triumphantly holding it aloft for us to see, but it was 15 minutes before we got permission to pass the signal at 'red' to go forward to Dorchester West Junction home signal. We stopped at the signal and, in accordance with Rule 55, it was necessary for the fireman to go to the signal box after waiting three minutes, to remind the signalman of the position of our train, but the snow was dead level with the footplate. 'Clive' looked at the snow, then at me, but he could not have climbed down or he would have disappeared from sight in snow over six feet deep. I gave a long blast on the whistle and the signalman, well aware of the situation, called out with a loud hailer, 'Stay where you are driver, we will have you as soon as we can free the points'.

A gang of platelayers were working to free the points in that appalling weather and it was 40 minutes before we were told to proceed, but in the comparative comfort of our 'West Country's' cab we were, indeed, fortunate that we had such good protection.

We made our way towards Weymouth through drifts up to 10 ft deep, and when we reached Upwey station the down platform was covered in snow as high as the coaches, and my arm was pushed back into the cab but, by contrast, the up platform was absolutely clear, swept clean by the wind. Here again we were given permission to pass the signal at danger as the snow had made it immovable, then it was on into Weymouth station after further delays at each signal.

By the time we arrived at Weymouth depot we had been on duty six hours and I asked for relief so that 'Clive' and I could have a cup of tea and a bite to eat. There were several men about so while we had a 20 minute break, our locomotive was turned and more coal taken as well as water.

The snow had stopped falling by now and we made our way back to the station only to experience more delay waiting for points to be cleared so that we could get on to our train. We should have left at 8.25 am but were exactly an hour late when we set off with the up London train. Now that it was daylight it was rather disturbing to be running through the country side with no visible sign that a railway track really existed in front of us, because even the marks of our down journey had been covered over.

We went through several deep drifts but the very nature of the snow was such that it did not impede our passage to any great degree, but it was still difficult to see and I had to constantly wipe my goggles clean. We only lost ten minutes getting back to Bournemouth where we had relief, but we were both cold, wet and very dirty. There were no buses running so I was faced with a three mile walk through deep snow and by the time I arrived home had been away for 14 hours, being fit for nothing but bed!

'Clive' was a good mate and we worked well together on any class of engine but, we came unstuck one day at Swanage when we were turning a Standard class '4' locomotive with a high sided tender. The tender was rather full of water and it was essential to balance the locomotive so that the turntable could be set in motion. As there is a retaining wall very close by, so as to be sure of not striking it with the front buffers it was necessary to move the locomotive further on to the turntable as soon as it started to revolve.

We had help from the station staff so 'Clive' directed me for this operation but, unfortunately, we had a steam blow and I lost sight of him at the crucial moment that he gave me the signal to stop. As soon as I saw it I slammed on the brake but too late and the back tender wheels landed on 'Old England' bringing us to an abrupt halt. We were now opposite the stone retaining wall so I decided that to avoid a lengthy delay I would try to re-rail the engine. Warning everyone to stand clear, I took the locomotive forward and much to my relief the back tender wheels mounted the table and I stopped just clear of the wall.

Securing the locomotive, I helped turn it round, then after checking that there was no damage, I set back on to our train enabling us to leave on time, thankful that my gamble had paid off.

We were allocated two Drewry 204 hp diesel mechanical shunting locomotives and I was given a short course in the yard at Christchurch, over a period of three days, to learn how to drive them and to detect faults that may occur. My previous experience on diesels in Canada had given me an advantage in the understanding of these locomotives and I knew that it would not be many years before they would be taking the place of steam, so I decided to study this form of traction for future reference.

Not long after learning these shunters I had serious back problems, suffering a slipped disc calling for hospital treatment, which left me encased in plaster from my pelvis to my neck. The railway doctor would not let me drive steam engines in this condition but he recommended that I should be given work as a second man on these diesels, so I was used in this capacity for the next five months.

Hospital treatment failed to remedy my problem but I heard of a man in Cornwall who was very adept at setting one's bones so, out of desperation, I went to see him. As if by some miracle he corrected my back in just a few minutes, making it possible for me to return to my own job of driving steam locomotives.

During this enforced absence from steam 'Clive' Brooker had been promoted to the next link and I now had a new fireman, Dougie Robinson, who lived at New Milton. Dougie was very inexperienced but he more than made up for lack of skill by his boundless energy and his willingness to learn, so we got along together very well. It is true that I had to keep an eye on him, offering advice when it was needed but never in a way that was likely to offend as I know only too well the effect that this can have on a young fireman.

Living at New Milton often meant that he had to catch a train down for our early turn well in advance of our signing on time, but he did not sit around waiting for time he would often do his own preparation work and my oiling as well, then greet me with a cup of tea when I arrived to sign on. In return I would help him out when we were disposing of engines, making sure that he did not miss a convenient train home. This kind of co-operation was the very essence of the job in steam days and brought men together in a bond of friendship that lasted throughout their careers.

We did a lot of preparation work which either had us working trains from Bournemouth West station to hand over to our own Top Link men or to the Nine Elms men and Dougie and I always made certain there was no cause for complaint from them. Alternatively, we would work down to Weymouth and back then hand over. We worked together to ensure that we had a good fire, plenty of well stacked coal available and a clean well swept footplate as well as a full head of steam. I cannot recall a single occasion when we did not hand over an engine in anything but the best of condition. Call it pride in the job if you will but a lot of it was personal satisfaction that the job had been well done.

One Nine Elms fireman had a go at Dougie, purely in fun, complaining that he had to start firing at Winchester after sitting down until then, so well had Dougie built up the fire.
Most Nine Elms men seemed to be full of that traditional cockney humour, often making light of adversity which was demonstrated to me on one occasion when I was learning the Waterloo road. The locomotive was a 'Merchant Navy' class and the crew were having a rough trip for steam, but this was not for want of effort on the part of the fireman. With the steam gauge back on 140 lb., out of desperation he took off his cloth cap and playfully hit the gauge with it saying 'Steam you B, steam'. Then suddenly burst into song with an 'I've got plenty of nothing' routine that brought a smile from the anxious driver taking all the tension out of the situation. Turning the top of the bank the situation gradually improved with the driver showing his knowledge of the road by coasting at every opportunity, thus successfully finishing the journey on time.
When the class '33' diesels entered service at Bournemouth, drivers had to go to the Traction Training School at Milford Goods Yard near Salisbury, which meant a long day for the senior men, but by the time it was my turn to learn them a new School had opened at Southampton. The course covered a period of three weeks to give us a good insight into the working of these diesels, also the ability to diagnose faults and to correct them, if possible.
This was a far cry from my first diesel course which was when I was in No. 1 Link firing to Frank Horn. The Southern introduced its first main line diesels during 1951, three in all, 10201, 10202 and 10203 and in company with driver Len 'Bow Bells' Hampton and fireman Dave Poole, we were sent up to Eastleigh works to bring the first one into service.
We were met by footplate inspector Len Willoughby and he gave us a brief run down on the layout of the locomotive; supplied us with typewritten instructions on how to drive them, detect faults and how to light and maintain the boiler for steam heating the coaches.
Under his watchful eye Frank started up No. 10202 then, having built up enough air, tested the brake, then took it out on to the train which was in the loop platform at Eastleigh. I coupled on to the train and then Len started to show both of us firemen how to ignite the burner in the boiler but no sooner had he shown us the igniter, which consisted of a form of poker into which a small firework was inserted, than he was called away by Mr Townroe, the motive power officer, to clear up a query he had. 'I'll get back to you as soon as I can', said Len, but we saw no more of him until we arrived at Southampton, where we backed into the down bay platform for 20 minutes. He came back to us and started his instruction all over again, only to be called away before he had finished the first sentence. So in desperation he handed us the instruction sheets and told us to sort it out for ourselves. That was the extent of our first lesson on diesels. On reading the instructions, we soon had the Spanner boiler going and the running of it presented us with no difficulties.
We spent the first week of our class '33' course studying in the classroom at Southampton. All of us in the class, six Salisbury drivers and six Bournemouth drivers, experienced considerable difficulty in absorbing all of the information imparted by our instructor, so different it was from our previous form of

traction, the steam locomotive.

The second week was spent out on the track working freight trains and here I found not the slightest difficulty, handling the diesel with ease and thoroughly enjoying every minute of it.

We were back in the classroom again for the third and final week and, having worked on the locomotives everything fell into place, thus making the written examination on the final day relatively simple. But still a few drivers did not pass and had to have the course extended so that they could clear up certain points they had failed to understand.

These locomotives were gradually introduced and I liked the power and the comfort of them but I disliked the smell of diesel fumes, also the noise of the engine. Knowing this was the motive power of the future I studied the text books so that I could fully understand them.

Dougie and I worked on together on both steam and diesels for a few more months then he was promoted so, once again, a good partnership was broken up.

My next mate was Bill Gallagher, a young lad from Northern Ireland who, like Dougie, was at first very inexperienced, but he also was willing to learn and did his best at all times. He did, however, have a tendency to lose his temper quite easily, not I hasten to add with me, but with the locomotive or his tools when things did not go right.

One occasion that I call to mind was one night when we were working the down Mail   which changed engines at Eastleigh. We had prepared our Standard class '4' locomotive No. 76019 at Eastleigh Loco Shed, but because of the smallness of the coal were unable to build up much of a fire, so this meant that Bill had to start firing as soon as we left Eastleigh station.

Bill raised the metal tender flap to get at the coal, securing it with the chain provided, but the hooks were bent downwards and as soon as he took the first shovelful of coal the flap came down across the shovel trapping it by the blade. Giving a grunt, Bill again lifted the flap then took another shoveful of coal, but alas down it came again and I could see Bill's temper beginning to well up. Furiously wrenching at the shovel he shook it from side to side to free it but it did not work, so up went the flap again, to be secured by the chain. Once again he tried but immediately down it came and this was more than Bill could stand, so he seized the flap handle with both hands lifting it clear of the guides then, spinning round, he threw the flap into his side front corner of the cab. Unfortunately, the damper wheel which was about 15 inches high was right in the flight path of the flying flap and it rebounded back landing right across both of Bill's feet. He let out a yell, then danced around the cab like a dervish uttering a string of swear words which would not have got past Mary Whitehouse.

The situation was so comical that I had to look out round the side of the cab so that he could not see me laughing, but I could not help myself. I felt a little ashamed later because I know that it must have hurt, but when we stopped at Southampton I tapped the hooks on the tender doors gently back into shape so that it could not happen again.

Bill soon regained his composure and set about the fire with gusto, giving us a good trip back to Bournemouth where we had relief by Weymouth men.

Our early days together were full of similar incidents, all of them less painful but still very amusing from my point of view at least, but Bill was one of those fortunate people able to laugh at themselves.

One day Bill asked me if I had seen the film on television the previous evening, so I replied, 'No, I never watch television!' 'Do you ever go to the cinema?', he asked, so I said, 'No, I never go to see a film!' Pursuing his line of questioning, he asked 'Don't you ever go to see a show or a Pantomime?'

Replying I said, 'No, I don't need to, I get all the entertainment I want just watching you!' He laughed at my words, knowing that there was no malice in them.

Bill would always follow my instructions and any advice that I gave him, so I taught him how to make the job easy, yet to get the best out of an engine, how to get coal round into the back corners of a 'Merchant Navy's' firebox, how to reach the front of a 'Lord Nelson's' long firebox and the best way to clean a fire without getting into a lather. Whenever Bill got into a tangle, and that became a rarity, I only had to point at his feet, drawing an imaginary line across them to remind him of his down Mail incident and he would laugh and cool down at once.

He soon became a good fireman and he was never afraid of hard work, but our days together did not last very long because the days of steam were rapidly drawing to a close, meaning the end of a way of life I had enjoyed for 28 years.

I knew I would miss the little things that meant so much, such as the way Bill would always produce two Penguin chocolate bars when we paused for a cup of tea, never failing to hand me one, in an act of friendship. I had, indeed, been very lucky in having so many good mates and I will never forget the numerous occasions that brought joy to my heart doing a job that was second to none.

Sunday 9th July, 1967 was our last day together on a trip to Weymouth and I just could not believe that this was steam's final day, as I felt sure that there would have to be some kind of run down but, I was wrong because as each engine finished its work, the fire was thrown out and it was stabled to await being towed away for breaking up. But happily some have survived to be lovingly restored and put back into service on private railways. Long may they live!

I had been on two courses around Christmas 1966, one to learn electric multiple units and the other to learn electro-diesel locomotives which were equipped to work in push and pull formation with unpowered four car units, or with powered and unpowered stock.

My first course on diesels had been a bit of a headache, but I found subsequent courses to be very absorbing and I had no difficulties in learning even the most complicated schematics. In fact, I progressed so well that I was offered a job as instructor but I decided that this was not for me because I did not relish the idea of being in a classroom most of the time and I did not want to give up driving.

I preferred to carry on doing the job that had brought me so much pleasure, but what I had failed to realize was the fact that, in the diesel and electric age, most of the time a driver worked alone, cutting out much of the very essence of the job, teamwork and true friendship as well as a sense of achievement at the end of each day.

Thick pot for cylinder oil

Chapter Eight

The New Beginning

The end of steam brought about many changes to Bournemouth Depot and our old system of Links of 12 pairs of men was abolished. We were reduced from a one time total of 107 pairs of men down to 70 drivers plus 30 secondmen, the new name for firemen.

We now had two Links. The top one consisted of 48 drivers doing main line work and the second Link of 18 drivers working on diesels or diesel electric multiple units, as well as 4 drivers solely on shunting duties at Bournemouth Carriage Sidings.

The secondmen were used where light engine running was necessary on shunting duties, or when overtime was involved, also if no meal break was rostered to the driver.

My seniority was sufficient to take me into the No. 1 Link and I was issued with a smart blue uniform which included shirts and a new style of cap.

Monday 10th July, 1967 marked the beginning of the completely new service and it was my lot to work the first local stopping train up to Waterloo. A Training School instructor was on hand to ride with me to see that everything ran smoothly.

I had a 4-car VEP unit built specially for high density traffic, having more seating capacity and a large number of doors for easy access. I had learned electric units seven months before, but I had never driven a VEP so this was a new experience for me. These units are fitted with a self lapping electro-pneumatic brake and up until then I had only been used to either a vacuum or air brake.

I was booked to stop at all stations to Woking, then Surbiton and finally Waterloo, so I took my time running into stations to get the feel of the brakes. After we had stopped at New Milton, the instructor said, 'Stan, you are only just timing the train, whereas you should really be waiting for time. That is because you are applying the brake too soon. When we run into Sway, don't apply the brake until I tell you, then give a full EP brake application, graduating it off as you are entering the station so as to stop smoothly'.

I shut off power as we were approaching Sway and applied the brake fully as soon as he told me to, but alarmingly we overran the station by four car lengths.

I propelled back into the station after receiving a hand signal from the guard and when we left we were now 3 minutes late so I said, 'Well Eric, we are now running late, so which is best?' 'Alright' said Eric, 'I won't say another word!' and he didn't, but in the next few weeks I realized what he meant, because as my braking technique improved I was, in fact, waiting for time at every station.

I found that if we were late for any reason, by rapidly attaining and constantly maintaining the maximum permitted speed and using the excellent EP brake, to its full advantage, it was possible to make up a lot of time and yet be able to stop smoothly.

The first time I was booked to work a fast train to Waterloo, stopping only at

Southampton, I just could not believe that it was possible to do the journey in 100 minutes, which was the booked time. Fast trains up until then had been allowed 2 hours 10 minutes for the same stops when hauled by a steam locomotive, and to reduce this time by 30 minutes was difficult for any one to comprehend.

I had not had any experience at driving a REP unit except under training conditions on special trains, and then only for brief periods of time. I was very impressed at the way the REP responded at the first touch of the controller, rapidly increasing speed so that I had to close the controller soon after Pokesdown as I was up to my maximum of 90 mph.

Braking hard to bring down the speed to 60 mph to run through Christchurch, I opened up again as I passed over the River Avon, climbing up towards Hinton Admiral at a speed that no steam engine could possibly have matched, again having to brake to obey the speed check there.

I found that the REP could coast for considerable distances, losing only very small amounts of speed and that the response to the EP brake was so good that with a touch it was possible just to lose the precise amount of speed required to conform to the permanent restrictions. Instead of having difficulty in maintaining time, in fact, the very opposite was the case, the problem being how to hold the unit back so as not to run before time.

Once by Litchfield tunnel it was a case of constantly letting the unit coast which, of course, keeps down the running cost.

The top permitted speed for the line was 90 mph as was the unit speed, so the miles were quickly swallowed up. The ride on these units was smooth and quiet compared to a steam locomotive, but the element that made steam so enjoyable was missing, that of teamwork. Quite a number of drivers did not take to the new forms of traction very easily and found the isolation of the driving cab to be almost intolerable.

It is not easy to describe the effects of being in a confined space, about 36 inches square, for, sometimes, up to three hours without any form of contact with the human race. In fact, it can be soul destroying and took a lot of getting used to.

Former driver Clive Groome, of Nine Elms and Waterloo, has written much on this subject in his excellent book *The Decline and Fall of the Engine Driver* and has summed it all up beautifully. I thoroughly agree with all that he has had to say on the subject!

There were many teething troubles in the first few weeks of electrification, some caused by inexperience but more often by incidents such as kick boards not being properly replaced, resulting in shoe gear being torn off, or failure to provide ramps at certain locations, resulting in the conductor rail being dislodged causing long delays.

I was very lucky during this troubled period, escaping without incident, but I have had my share of problems caused by broken shoe arms. The REP units were fitted with 16 shoes, all of which were inter-connected and I had my first incident one morning just as I was leaving Woking on an up semi-fast train. As I was pulling out of the station with REP 3007, there was a massive short on the leading left hand side shoes and immediately the line indicator went to 'off', telling me that I had lost traction current.

Opening my side window, I heard a dragging noise then, as the traction current was restored there was a second short and off went the line light again. There was a signal a close distance ahead, so I coasted up to it and informed the signalman that I had lost the leading shoe arm and would deal with it as soon as possible. Luckily, the damaged shoe gear was over a gap in the live rail so I decided not to have the traction current isolated and with the help of the guard, Jack Bartlett, I cut out the unit and then lifted the shoes clear of the live rail, isolating them with shoe paddles. I insulated the broken lead with tape from the emergency tool cupboard and in just 14 minutes we were on our way and arrived in Waterloo just 10 minutes late, having regained 4 minutes *en route*.

The new service from Waterloo to Weymouth was worked in the following manner. On leaving Waterloo the train was formed of 2 four car TC unpowered units and the REP unit, a 4 car set of 3200 hp, bringing up the rear. Leaving Waterloo on the half hour with only one stop at Southampton, the time allowed was 100 minutes for the 108 miles. On arrival at Bournemouth the driver vented out the air in the brake valve and removed his key, without which a unit could not be moved.

He then walked back to the REP unit where a shunter was waiting and after inserting his key he detached that unit. In the meantime a Crompton class '33' fitted for push and pull working came out of the siding on to the front of the train, stopping short until the rear end shunter gave the tip that the detachment had been completed. A second shunter now attached the class '33' to the train then, after the guard had tested the brake, the train completed the journey to Weymouth. Diesels had to be used for the Bournemouth to Weymouth section because the line was only electrified as far as Branksome, some 2 miles west of Bournemouth.

Soon after I retired, the whole of this remaining 34 miles was electrified and new '442' class units were placed into service. These units consisted of five cars and the motors of the REP units were used to power them, having proved to be very reliable in the previous 20 years.

I was authorised to drive a variety of forms of traction, namely all types of electric multiple units, class '33s', class '47s' diesel electrics and class '73' and '74' electro diesels which are essentially an electric locomotive but fitted with a small diesel engine for movement over sections of the line that are not electrified. I also learned three types of shunting locomotives. The 204 hp Drewry diesel mechanical, the 275 hp Ruston & Hornsby and the 350 hp '08' and '09' classes of diesel electrics. All of these locomotives were allocated to Bournemouth and covered the shunting work at Bournemouth Goods Yard, Bournemouth station and Poole Yard.

They were also used on the line to Hamworthy Goods, working light freight trains and covering the shunting work which, at times, was quite considerable. On these turns they were manned by two men owing to the fact that we had to work over road crossings and shared the dock area with all kinds of road transport so, in the interests of safety, a second man was always there.

As in steam days, there was a day that, on reflection, must have been my worst day for a chain of events that could not have been foreseen. This occurred on a duty, a special, that, on paper, could not have been easier.

With secondman Tom Upshall as my mate, our duty was as follows to relieve a freight train at Bournemouth, work it to Totton Yard, then run light with the class '33' to Southampton, pick up four cars off the back of a down London train and take them into Southampton Docks with passengers for the QE2.

After unloading, we had to take the four cars to Eastleigh empty to connect with a down semi-fast to Bournemouth which was booked to terminate at Eastleigh as track work in the Christchurch area called for the traction current to be isolated.

The passengers were to be transferred to our train to complete their journey to Bournemouth. Right from the start things did not run smoothly because the freight train arrived with the wrong type of class '33' locomotive, one not fitted for push and pull working. We worked the freight to Totton Yard then I contacted the running foreman at Eastleigh requesting a push and pull fitted engine. He told told my to bring my locomotive to the Depot and then take No. 33119 back to Southampton to complete my duty. So we did as we were instructed. However, on arrival at Southampton we were requested to contact the signalman at once. I phoned him and he said, 'Driver, there is a failed class '47' in the up slow and I want you to pull it off its train, place it in the up sidings then your engine will be used to work the train through to its destination'. So, after making the shunt, we gave up our locomotive to the crew of the '47'.

Again I got in touch with the Eastleigh running foreman who informed me that a parcels train was on its way up from Bournemouth hauled by two class '73' electro-diesels working in multiple under the control of one driver. 'Take the first ED off that train, then complete your duty with it', he said. So, having 30 minutes to wait we made a cup of tea and had a bite to eat.

When the EDs arrived, we took No. 73114 from the front of the parcels train and crossed over to the down holding siding to await the arrival of the Boat train 4-car unit. It was now late evening and the temperature was below freezing point, with a white frost beginning to show on the sleepers. I realized that the ED would not be able to provide heat and light to the train once we had left the live rail, but reasoned that there would be no delay so the period without heat would be minimal.

Once we had arrived in the Docks, we were stopped short of the unloading platform and the shunter informed me that there would be a 40 minute wait. I told him that the passengers could not sit in unheated coaches without lights for that length of time and Control would have to be told of the circumstances. He soon returned and told me that Control had instructed him to deal with my train as soon as possible. We were to push the vans which were being unloaded in the platform out of the way, get the passengers out, and then reposition the vans. After that we would be released for our down train from Eastleigh.

We were on our way to Eastleigh in less than 15 minutes, arriving at the up platform where we were met by the running foreman. 'Sorry', he said, 'but I will have to pinch your ED as we need it to work a train to Chichester', adding, 'A class '33' has just left the Depot, it will come out on your train so that you won't be late away'.

No. 33108 arrived and it was evident that it had only just been released from the Works as it had been overhauled and was really gleaming with its new coat of paint.

We left right on the dot, our first stop being Southampton, then Brockenhurst, but as I was about to close the controller for the speed restriction round Wood Fidley curve there was a loud bang from the engine room and the amp gauge fell to zero.

I turned to Tom saying, 'There goes our main generator field circuit breaker!' He went back to reset it. I tried the controller to make sure we had power again, then satisfied, closed it as we were approaching Brockenhurst and had sufficient speed to coast comfortably into the station.

When I got the 'right away' from the guard, I opened the controller and pulled steadily out of the station but, when the amp gauge reached 1,000 amps, we suddenly lost power, so I closed it again but this time the main generator field did not trip. Closing the controller automatically resets overloads and when I re-opened it, I again had power, but this time we had a another overload at 900 amps; and so it went on, with less amps being reached with each one. However, I managed to reach New Milton with little loss of time owing to our light load. Pulling away from the station proved to be another series of opening and closing the controller until finally we lost power altogether, but we had managed to reach the down grade just before Hinton Admiral so I knew we would have no difficulty in coasting into Christchurch.

With Tom's co-operation, we tried a series of motor isolations but, to no avail. So I had no alternative but to request assistance as soon as we stopped in the platform. To my dismay I was informed that there would be a long delay as there was no crew available to bring an assisting locomotive out to us. I told the guard, then I checked through the fault and failure procedures to see if I had overlooked anything, but no, everything that could be done had been done so we settled down for a long wait. Fortunately the diesel engine was still running so we were able to provide heat and light on that bitterly cold evening.

The delay was not as long as I had expected because the relief crew lost no time in getting up to the depot after they signed on duty quickly preparing a class '33', then setting out for Christchurch.

Coming in behind us via the crossover which existed at the time, the attachment was made, then after testing the brake I was able to drive from our failed engine, having previously isolated the engine control switch.

On examining the locomotive later the Depot maintenance staff found that we had had a flashover on the main generator and that there were faults on three out of the four traction motors, probably caused by small pieces of metal that had entered the motor casings during the overhaul.

I heard no more of the matter but Tom and I have often talked about that day and the series of events that took place making it the worst day that I can remember whilst working on diesel locomotives. But it is fair comment to say that during the 20 years and more that I did work on them failures were few and far between.

I was much happier working on electric multiple units as I could never really get used to the noise and smell of diesels. One good thing about diesels was that you often had a secondman and this eliminated the feeling of isolation that persisted when driving emus.

The only time that any difficulties were experienced when in charge of an emu was during very cold and icy conditions. Severe frost proved to be the worst of all. Perhaps the fact that our weather is so unpredictable caught us out on a few occasions. These occurred after de-icer trains had been sent out to coat the conductor rail with special de-icing fluid which was of an oily nature and, having completed their task, had returned to the Depot. Rain then fell and on coming into contact with this oily substance had run into globules of water which, owing to the rapidly falling temperatures had turned to ice, creating patterns which stood well above the rail level.

These ice patterns were a form of insulation which caused violent arcs of the traction current, that gave off intense white light and loud crackling noises. This light was further intensified by the frost covered trees and the effect on one's eyes was painful to say the least. When these conditions were severe enough the line indicator was constantly flicking 'on' and 'off', and the interruptions to the flow of traction current caused heat to generate at the collector shoes accompanied by thick yellow smoke. This, in turn, could cause the shoes and shoe leads to become burnt, then the insulation around them to melt, resulting in a real danger of fire.

I recall one such occasion when I was working the 6.23 am Bournemouth to Waterloo which was formed of a 4-car VEP unit but was booked on arrival at Southampton to have an additional 8 cars attached which had run non-stop from Bournemouth and the two trains were combined at that station.

I experienced bad arcing but despite this kept fairly good time to Southampton where a short delay occurred waiting for the rear portion. After the attachment had been made on the rear and I had made the necessary brake test, we left seven minutes late.

With the additional VEP sets, I experienced a certain amount of buffeting but, made fairly good time, although plagued by constant arcing. By now it was becoming daylight and the pressure on my eyes eased somewhat.

I had a further few minutes delay waiting for the signal to clear at Basingstoke but, as I left I could see that conditions were now far worse, with the conductor rail literally coated in ice and progess became very erratic.

After several signal checks I was finally brought to a halt and in the distance I could see a train which was wreathed in smoke. Without delay, I phoned the signalman who told me that there was a train in the section ahead but he had not yet heard from its driver.

I told him I could see the train and it was obvious that he had a fire problem and was, no doubt, dealing with that first. I then went on to inform him that I would remain by the phone if he wanted to call me back.

Thanking me he said he would get back to me as soon as he had any information.

After 15 minutes, during which time I called the signalman to see if he had any information, I saw the guard of the train in front walking back towards me so I told the signalman this.

The guard explained that his train, which was formed of a REP and 8 TC coaches, had fires on the shoe leads and the delay had been caused by dealing with them first. The train was a complete failure and in need of assistance so, I was given permission to pass the signal at 'Red' and proceed to the rear of the train to propel it through to Woking.

The driver, who was waiting at the rear of the train, told me that he had badly burnt shoe leads and that he had cut the unit out and would rejoin the front cab of his train ready to be propelled on to Woking. He would control the brake, but owing to the rail conditions would not try to drive my unit from the front but would leave that to me.

I asked him if he had tied up the shoes as REP units are not fitted with shoe fuses but, much to my surprise, he said he had not. I said, 'I think you will find that you will have to, because leads are still able to pick up current although your unit is isolated, but we can try first.'

On receiving his signal to start I opened the controller cautiously but, after only a few feet there was a short circuit from his unit and the traction current circuit breaker tripped out.

I contacted him on the Loudaphone and said, 'It's no good Ted, your shoes will have to be tied up, I'll secure my unit then come up to help you to do it. In the meantime get on to the electrical controller and get the "juice" cut off again'.

He returned from the phone and assured me that the 'juice' was, indeed, off and we set to work to tie up the 16 shoes fitted to the REP. This was a long and laborious task, especially as we only had thick rope which needed to be stranded to make it possible to tie knots in it and it required the two of us to do each one.

On completing the task, Ted went off to get the current restored while I placed the unused rope back in the emergency cupboard and the shoe paddles back in the REP, then went back to the cab of the VEP ready for the off.

For the second time I received Ted's ready to start signal and started away again, half expecting trouble but, apart from the arcing from my shoes, we were all right, as I cautiously drove the 24 coaches towards Woking.

The gradient is slightly downhill for most of the way and I coasted at every opportunity, but after a few miles we lost traction current again and we found we had to re-tie some of the shoes as the ice that was on the conductor rail had severed the cords.

Again the 'juice' had to be cut off and more delay was inevitable while we carried out the necessary work but, by now, time had ceased to have any real importance as we were hours adrift. In fact, we arrived in Woking at exactly the time that I should have been arriving back at Bournemouth and having a 30 minute meal break.

Ted and I both had relief and went over to the mess room for a most welcome cup of tea, having signed on six hours earlier, then we went back to Bournemouth 'on the cushions' as our trains had passed us while we were still going 'up'.

Several trains had had problems. One, a VEP, had burnt out its shoe leads at Fleet and another at Brookwood. The weather had been responsible for what proved to be a very expensive day for British Rail's Southern Region.

Snow can also be a big problem, especially if it is of the drier, powdery kind because this has a tendency to enter into the motor generator units causing them to short out, blowing fuses or doing far greater damage.

It is, indeed, fortunate that we rarely have winters like the one of 1962-3 because if we did I am afraid that the former Southern Region, with its third rail system, would suffer very badly with widespread disruption to its services and damage to its equipment.

It is not only the weather that causes damage to equipment because quite often, and sometimes with tragic results, this is brought about by the mindless vandalism of the worst kind.

One night I was running down towards Christchurch on a de-icer train in weather that was several degrees below freezing and everthing was white with frost. We were making good time and the thought ran through my mind that I would soon be home in bed, but as if designed to shatter those thoughts, my line indicator went to 'off' and I lost traction current.

I coasted down into Christchurch expecting it to return at any moment but, when it did not, I decided to stop at the signal in the station rather than trust to luck that it would be restored.

The signalman informed me that something was causing a dead short and that a class '33' loco was just leaving Bournmemouth with a van train and would examine the line *en route* to ascertain the cause. In the meantime, the line indicator had flicked 'on' then 'off' again a couple of times, indicating that the cause of the problem was still very much with us.

My de-icer unit was an old 'Sub' stock 2-car set and with no power coming into it I had lost heating and my lights were back on to battery power. My compressors had stopped and I was rapidly losing air pressure for my brakes, so I wound on my hand brake, then we were suddenly plunged into darkness as the depleted battery could not retain the lights. I placed my 'Bardic' lamp on the front of the unit as my headlight had also gone out.

The class '33' arrived alongside us and the driver said that they had searched the line but, had not been able to ascertain the cause of the problem but would let the signalman at Bournemouth know so that the line could be searched again. In the meantime we would just have to sit it out waiting for other arrangements to be made. I was thankful that I had a top coat as by now the cold was really beginning to bite.

The phone rang and the signalman informed me that an '09' shunting diesel was just about to leave the up platform at Bournemouth and the driver would be accompanied by a shunter to examine the line again. In due course the '09' arrived but, they had still been unable to locate the cause of the short so, they would return again over the same line to look again.

They were running through Pokesdown when a bright flash lit up the track behind them as the Electrical Controller tried again to restore the current. Dropping back to the spot clearly indicated by the smoke, they found that someone had thrown a metal road nameplate down on the line from the footbridge; the square section pole was down in between the running rail and the third rail causing a dead short.

Contacting the Controller they asked for his assurance that the current would not be tried again, then set to work to extract the pole which had become welded between the two rails. With the aid of a crowbar they managed to prise it loose, noting that the aluminium nameplate had melted into what looked like molten solder and that a chunk of the third rail had been burnt out but, it was still safe to travel over.

The first indication we had of this was when our motor generator suddenly burst into life and the compressor started to pound away building up our air pressure, so that we were soon able to have a brake test and get under way.

Happy to be moving again, but so very cold, it was good to know that soon we would, indeed, be able to get home to bed with my watch moving round towards 3.00 am.

Let it not be thought that my career on the footplate or, in the cab, has been a series of disasters because it must be remembered that it spans well over 50 years and, God willing, I hope it will continue for a few more years yet.

British Rail has changed almost beyond recognition over the past 50 years. Gone are the steam locomotives, and many miles of track, mostly under Beeching's axe, although many more have been lost since. Gone also are many thousands of freight wagons and coaches too, but out of all this has emerged a modern railway.

There is no doubt that it is faster, cleaner and more efficient than it was in steam days, but in terms of human relationships and job satisfaction, it has lost so much. One has only to be involved with a preservation railway to realize just how much has changed in this respect, because the atmosphere at these sites is a magical transformation back to what railways were in the past.

Modernisation has its vulnerable points as the early snow of 1991 showed. It has been argued that this was a 'particular' type of snow which brought the railways almost to a standstill. But, thinking back to 1962-3, the snow was so deep that at one cutting it actually came in through the roof vent of a 'West Country' class locomotive, yet did not prevent us from finishing our journey to Weymouth. I shudder to think what would have happened to an electric multiple unit faced with the same conditions.

However, when things are running normally one cannot question the fact that great progess has been made in the speed of trains in general and in the degree of comfort provided.

SWANAGE RAILWAY
Driver Training
Steam Locomotive Familiarisation

Locomotive Class/Type _A3 FLYING SCOTSMAN_ No. _60103_.

Item	Description	Completed Yes	No
1	General appreciation of engine.	✓	
2	Cab controls and their operation.	✓	
3	Additional equipment and its operation. Specify:	—	
4	Atomiser/hydrostatic lubricator operation.	✓	
5	All lubrication points and grades of lubricants.	✓	
6	Handling: driving and firing methods.	✓	
7.	Disposal Arrangements.	✓	
8	Guidance Notes issued?	—	
9	Light-engine movements to get 'feel' of engine	✓	
10	Driver accompanied on first train worked?	✓	

Instructors comments: _who am I - to teach this Gentleman_

Instructors signature _R. Kennington_ Date _16 July 94_

Name(print) _R. KENNINGTON_

I, the undersigned, hereby confirm that I have today received instruction on the class of locomotive stated above, and am confident to take charge of such class of locomotive:
Signed _S. Symes_ Date _16 July 1994_

Name(print) _STAN SYMES._

Chapter Nine

Back to Steam

Late in 1980, Jack Hookey, one of our train crew supervisors asked me if I would consider starting a Mutual Improvement Class for the drivers and firemen of the Swanage Railway, as they were in need of someone experienced at driving steam locomotives, as well as being conversant with rules and regulations.

He knew that I had taken such classes before and, after giving the matter some serious thought, I decided that I would have a go. It was with a certain amount of uneasiness that I held the first class because it was almost 14 years since I had last worked on steam and, thinking it was the last time I would do so, I had more or less dispelled the steam locomotive from my mind.

Much to my surprise all that I had learned in the past came flooding back to me and I knew I could do a lot to help these very enthusiastic men. I was impressed by their willingness to learn and, by using a casual method of teaching, I found that most of them made great strides. They were soon able to answer my questions with little difficulty as we gradually worked our way through the Rule Book then the British Transport Commission's *Handbook for Railway Steam Locomotive Enginemen* issued to all footplate men in steam days.

As in all classes, there were some who learned quickly and some who took a little longer. I made certain to keep pace with the slowest, coaxing the answers out of them until I was sure that they would have no difficulty when it was their turn to pass the inspector, George Elliot, a former footplate inspector of British Rail, retired, but still acting in that capacity for the Swanage Railway.

At this stage the railway only had small industrial locomotives and, frankly, I could just not interest myself in the practical side of driving these engines, declining all invitations to visit Swanage to try my hand at the controls.

However, I was at Swanage one Sunday and decided to call in at the station to see for myself just how much they had achieved in the re-building of their beloved railway. To say that I was surprised is a masterpiece of understatement as I was, in fact, truly amazed at just how much this group of amateurs had accomplished.

I mean no disrepect when I use the term amateurs but few, if any, had any railway experience, but all of them were fired with an enthusiasm that had to be seen to be believed. These men, and women, had turned the desolate waste that had once been a thriving railway back into a close copy of what I remembered, spending hours of their time voluntarily to do so.

My thoughts went back immediately to my early railway days during the war when everyone worked with a common purpose and co-operation was the very essence of life.

The fireman that day at Swanage was David Cash, who was the Chairman of the Swanage Railway. He was in the act of uncoupling No. 21 from his train and at once I noticed that he was about to start turning the coupler screw the wrong way, so I quietly said, 'I would try turning that the other way if I were you!'

He looked up surprised, then greeting me with a cheery smile said, 'Hello Stan, you have come to see us at last!' expressed with a warmth that made my day.

The driver, Mike Hoskin, asked me if I was coming for a ride on the footplate then, and, getting the smell of the locomotive in my nostrils, I found that I could not resist what was to me a trip back into the past.

When the guard blew his whistle Mike said, 'There you are she is all yours, have a go!' After a moment's hesitation I took over and, after looking at the road ahead, I blew the whistle, then eased open the regulator for a smooth pull out of the platform. No. 21 responded well and the 1 mile to Herston was soon covered, then as we approached the station I closed the regulator and gently applied the vacuum brake bringing the train quietly to a halt. It was a delight to be in control of a steam locomotive again, small though it may have been.

We ran around the train in readiness for our return to Swanage and on our arrival there I thanked both Mike and David saying, 'I did enjoy that, it brought back memories too precious to forget'.

They both asked when I was going to go on the roster as a driver but I would give no assurance on that as I was still working full time for British Rail. I did, however, visit from time to time and was never able to resist the offer to 'have a go'.

I held classes regularly every fortnight for six years up until it was time for me to retire from British Rail on 2nd October, 1987. It had been my intention to make a complete break from any form of railway connection but I was asked to go back to Swanage soon after that date as they wanted to make me a 'small presentation for my help in the past'.

My wife, Joan, and I went down to Swanage at the invitation of David Cash and, when we arrived, they had laid on a buffet lunch for us in the dining car. I was presented with a beautiful print of Cuneo's 'Merchant Navy' class No. 35027 *Port Line*, my old locomotive, signed by the artist, also a print of a watercolour by Eric Bottomley with 'M7' tank No. 30053 standing in the platform at Swanage. This was also signed by the artist with the words, 'to Stan Symes from Eric Bottomley'.

They also gave me a copy of the book *The Swanage Branch*, and a framed photograph of me standing on the front of No. 30053 on the day she returned to Swanage from the United States, both being the work of Andrew Wright the official photographer of the Swanage Railway. The book was signed by Andrew with the words, 'To Stan with best wishes on your retirement and all the best for the future. Andrew and everyone on the Swanage Railway 11.10.87'.

Finally, Mike Stollery, Chairman of the Southern Steam Trust, awarded me Honorary Life Membership of that trust with the following inscription:

Dear Stan,

As a token of our appreciation of all the time you have spent with the training of Swanage Railway Footplate Staff and all the help and encouragement you have so willingly given over the years the trustees are delighted to award you Honorary Life

BR Standard class '5MT' 4-6-0 No. 73020 is seen passing Bournemouth depot with a coal train from Poole en route to Bournemouth goods yard, 14th April, 1960. *Roy Panting*

The classic view of Bournemouth depot with its lifting gear and water softener from the down platform, 22nd September, 1957. The locomotives on shed are (from left to right) 'Merchant Navy' class 4-6-2 No. 35005 *Canadian Pacific*, 'Battle of Britain' class 4-6-2 No. 34110 *66 Squadron*, 'M7' class 0-4-4T No. 30111, 'G6' class No. 30260 and 'M7' class No. 30128. *Roy Panting*

A diesel-hauled down 'Bournemouth Belle' approaches Gas Works Junction near Branksome on 19th March, 1967. The engine is diesel electric Brush Type '4' class '47' Co-Co No. D1912. *Roy Panting*

'M7' class 0-4-4T No. 30058 on the rear of a push and pull train at Parkstone destined for Bournemouth West. *Robin White*

Re-routed due to permanent way work via Ringwood and the 'Old Road' the 'Bournemouth Belle' headed by 'West Country' class 4-6-2 No. 34009 *Lyme Regis* and with banking assistance, starts its climb of Parkstone bank, 3rd April, 1960.   *Roy Panting*

'Battle of Britain' class 4-6-2 No. 34073 *249 Squadron* rounds the curve between the two level crossing gates at Poole with the 12.35 pm Waterloo-Weymouth, 24th August, 1963. *Roy Panting*

'King Arthur' class 4-6-0 *Sir Urre of the Mount* about to leave Poole on an up Weymouth train on 14th June, 1960.   *Colin Stone*

'Merchant Navy' class 4-6-2 No. 35025 *Brocklebank Line* waits for the signal to be raised on the up line at Poole station.   *Robin White*

The 'Bug', Adams 'B4' class 0-4-0T No. 30093 with a train of coal leaving Poole Quay. These engines were ideal dockside locomotives being small but very strong. *R. Smith Collection*

Class '3MT' 2-6-2T No. 82026 crosses the River Stour as it approaches Wimborne with the 2.25 pm Bournemouth West-Brockenhurst train, 30th April, 1964. *Author*

'Battle of Britain' class 4-6-2 No. 34063 *229 Squadron* is seen at Wimborne with a train for Salisbury via West Moors and Fordingbridge, June 1963.   *Author*

BR Standard class '3MT' 2-6-2T No. 82029 runs into Ringwood on the down 11.04 am Brockenhurst-Bournemouth Central train with a 2-car push and pull set on 4th April, 1964. These locomotives replaced Drummond's 'M7s' on this service. However they were not 'push-pull' fitted.   *C.L. Caddy Collection*

'U' class 2-6-0 No. 31792 runs into Daggons Road station on the 9.23 am Salisbury-Bournemouth West train which ran via West Moors, 2nd May, 1964.   *C.L. Caddy Collection*

Bournemouth Central's former regular shunting engine 'M7' class 0-4-4T No. 30112 is seen on the 12.10 pm Weymouth- Bournemouth Central local train at Holton Heath station. An unusual duty for this class of locomotive, 3rd October, 1960.   *Roy Panting*

'M7' class 0-4-4T No. 30060 is ready to leave the bay platform at Wareham for Swanage with a 2-car push and pull set in April 1958. The driver will control the train from the leading coach using controls operated by compressed air to work the engine's regulator. The Westinghouse pump which provides the compressed air can be clearly seen attached to the smokebox.

W. Reed

Ex-LMS Ivatt class '2MT' 2-6-2T No. 41316 passes Swanage engine shed with the 12.21 pm from Wareham. These locomotives were ideal for this job, 31st August, 1966.   *Roy Panting*

Membership of the Southern Steam Trust.
The trustees and members extend their warmest wishes for your retirement from British Railways and look forward to a long and continuing association with you on the Purbeck Line.

Sincerely Mike Stollery
10th October, 1987

On reading these messages, my resolution to cut all railway ties immediately dissolved. Within a short speech of thanks I told the large gathering of this resolve, but gave an assurance that I would continue teaching new footplate staff and would now stand in as driver when needed for as long as I was able.

My wife was presented with a large box of chocolates and we went on a ride on the 2 pm from Swanage to Herston, Joan in the train and me, again, at the controls of No. 21.

One task I had undertaken was to train all of the Swanage drivers on the '08' class 350 hp diesel electric shunting locomotive No. D3591 that they had purchased from British Rail in good running order.

Coupled to the first train, in front of No. 21, I drove the diesel up to Herston. After being uncoupled, I ran forward onto the next section of the line, still under construction, opening the catch points behind the locomotive to protect the operating line.

Being safely locked into the 'dead' section of the line, I took three drivers at a time then, after instructing them on their preparation duties, I made sure that each in turn knew the position of the various parts of the locomotive and went through the fault and failure procedures necessary in the event of a breakdown. Then I took the controls and explained the 'do's' and 'don'ts' of driving these excellent little locomotives, giving each one a session at driving using both air and vacuum brakes to simulate varying types of train. We had been through the clasroom stage of their tuition prior to this so they were, on paper at least, well acquainted with them.

I managed to teach nine drivers the practical side of these locomotives on that day, then, at our next M.I. class questioned each in turn to make sure that they had fully understood such items as fuse changing, filter changeover procedures, header tank filling and numerous other necessary acts.

This locomotive proved invaluable during the construction of the line to Harman's Cross and will no doubt give good service as we press on to Corfe Castle.

My next session of practical training was to acquaint train crews with the line from Herston to Harman's Cross, learning crossings, speed restrictions and procedures to be carried out when running around the train at Harman's Cross. On the first day of training, former Midland Railway class '1F' locomotive No. 41708 was lit up in readiness for the duty but, when she had sufficient steam, we found that it was impossible to work either injector so the fire had to thrown out and the '08' was pressed into service.

These trips gave some of the drivers a chance to learn the gradients but using the '08' did not give a true picture of what to expect when working a train hauled by a steam locomotive.

In my capacity as Training Officer, I was in attendance when, on Saturday 19th November, 1988, we ran our first crew training passenger train empty to Harman's Cross. Leaving Swanage at 10.00 am the 4-coach train was hauled by the class '08'.

We had hoped to check the timings for the run but the '08' proved to be too slow, especially when pulling away after slowing down for the farm crossings, so we had no way of being sure that they were practical.

On our next trip we had the class '1F' 0-6-0 No. 41708 driven by Nick Hanham and fired by Dave Round, so now was our chance to see if it was possible to keep to the booked time. Before leaving Swanage, it was suggested that, as it was 'Save the Children Week', any driver that made the wheels slip or any fireman who ran out of steam should place £1 in the collection box and this was readily agreed to by all.

We left at 11.00 am and Nick pulled steadily out of the station, making certain that he did not allow No. 41708 to slip. Having been standing with the dampers closed for a long time, the engine did not respond to Dave's efforts and the steam pressure fell back to 120 lb. without the injector being used, until Nick shut off the steam for Herston. We ran into the station with half a glass of water, and no increase in boiler pressure, so when the water rose to ¾-full Dave shut off the injector to allow the boiler pressure to build up.

By now the guard was blowing his whistle, so Nick acknowledged his signal but waited until he had built up another 10 lb. of steam pressure. Pulling away slowly, Nick pulled the lever up and gave No. 41708 plenty of regulator whilst Dave was busy with the shovel. When I glanced at the fire I could see that it was not burning as brightly as it should have been. Even the use of the 'pricker' failed to liven up the fire.

With boiler pressure still at 130 lb. it was now time to put the injector on, which had an immediate effect on the boiler pressure and it fell back quite quickly, causing the vacuum to fall back as well.

The gradient out of Swanage is rising all the way to Harman's Cross except for a short length through the station at Herston, so there is nowhere that it is possible to shut off steam and coast. Dave shut off the injector in an attempt to raise the boiler pressure. Despite his efforts the boiler pressure and vacuum soon fell and the train ground to a halt on the 1 in 76 bank.

We waited until he had sufficient steam pressure to get the brake off fully, then had another go, this time just managing to reach the station at Harman's Cross but, again, in a much depleted state for steam and water.

With the boiler pressure up to 140 lb. and half a glass of water, we ran around the train and were soon on our way back to Swanage. To give Dave his due, he donated £1 to the 'Save the Children' Fund with a good heart, but was not at all happy with running short of steam.

While we were taking water Dave cleaned the fire. When the tank was full we set back onto our train and Nick coupled up whilst Dave hastily made up his fire in readiness for the next trip.

We started away when the guard gave the 'tip' but the fire was still green, so Nick gave No. 41708 plenty of regulator to liven it up. Although this had the desired effect, when we ran into Herston the water level was well down.

We were well over our booked time filling the boiler to a reasonable level but as the train was not conveying passengers this was not important.

Nick decided to leave Herston when we had ¾ of a glass of water and the steam was creeping up to 135 lb. on the gauge. We pulled out of Herston and Dave used the 'little and often' method of firing but the fire was still not hot enough. However, we did manage to crawl into Harman's Cross station, again low in steam and water.

By the time we had run-round the train the fire was just about right and on the down grade back to Swanage Dave managed to get back a good glass of water.

Handing over on arrival to driver Ron Roberts, a former British Rail fireman, Nick gave him a briefing on the two trips and wished him luck, but it was obvious to me that the fire was now ready for the off. I had a few words with fireman Chris Castro, advising him to put the injector on soon after leaving Swanage, and to feed the fire steadily, keeping it hot so as to maintain a good working boiler pressure.

Chris started firing as soon as we left Swanage station and No. 41708 responded immediately with the needle moving towards the red line, so on went the injector but this time there was no drop in pressure, which brought a smile to Ron's face. The brief stop at Herston allowed us to top up the boiler before we were off for the next leg of the journey. Ron was working No. 41708 as lightly as possible, yet ensuring that he kept time. No difficulty arose which was a relief as there had been some doubt in my mind as to whether the trip was too much for the '1F' hauling five coaches. We ran into Harman's Cross with half a glass of water and the steam pressure just below the red line, giving Chris control over the boiler while we ran around the train.

The next two trips were similar and showed that good management of the locomotive is essential if timing of the train is to be achieved with these small engines.

The first passenger carrying train to run to Harman's Cross was at 2.15 pm on Saturday 3rd December, 1988 and it was a Special conveying Premier Life Members of the Swanage Steam Trust. The train was double headed by 'Jinty' No. 47383 on loan from the Severn Valley Railway, and '1F' No. 41708. I was driving the 'Jinty' and Malcolm Collop, who is now a driver on British Rail, was my fireman and Ron Roberts was driving with Dave Round firing No. 41708.

We left Swanage with a 7-coach train; we received a tremendous welcome at Harman's Cross and were the subject of literally hundreds of photographs.

We ran-round the train and every inch of our shunt must be on record as cameras were constantly clicking. When we arrived back at Swanage we had a second trip to do and this time all of our passengers were members of the Southern Electric Group.

The 'Jinty' was an excellent locomotive to work on and this was the first time I had driven one of this class. Smaller locomotives had been previously used on the Swanage line but with the extension of the track the 'Jinty' was most certainly the type of engine needed for the long uphill pull and she did so magnificently.

I am sure that at times we were also pulling No. 41708 as well as the train as it was not steaming too well, due to poor quality coal.

We were all sorry to have to part with No. 47383 but it was needed back on the Severn Valley line, but maybe she will come back one day, who knows!

The next engine we had on loan was a GWR Pannier Tank No. 7752 which had previously been the property of the London Underground, but is now owned by the Birmingham Railway Museum at Tyseley. She was designed by Collett and built in 1930 by the North British Locomotive Co. with a boiler pressure of 200 lb. and a weight of 47½ tons.

Beautifully painted in GWR green with brass safety valve cover, she has been a big attraction at Swanage. She is nice to drive but when it comes to oiling one needs to be somewhat of a contortionist to get at some of the missionary boxes and corks. She has proved to be a real work horse and without her we would probably have had to revert to diesel power in the form of the class '08'.

During the summer of 1989 we also had on loan from the Severn Valley Railway the Ivatt '2MT' tender locomotive No. 46443, a 2-6-0 which was ideally suited to the Swanage Line.

To date this locomotive is easily my favourite, with ample power, a good size cab and the added advantage of a rocking and drop grate making it possible to clean the fire in a few minutes with the very minimum of effort. She would run comfortably all day on a tender full of water, had an excellent lookout, would steam like a 'Black Five' and, as far as I am concerned, had no vices. She could be oiled in a quarter of the time it took to do the Pannier, and one could work on her for a week without soiling one's overalls!

I had a great time during the Christmas period of 1989, when I spent two days driving 'Santa Specials'. I believe a good time was had by all the 13,000 passengers we carried during the month of December.

Since I have retired I have been involved in a number of special occasions which have given me a great deal of pleasure. The first was when on Sunday 13th March, 1988 I was asked to take part in a BBC TV documentary programme entitled 'Back Tracking on Beeching', which dealt with the aftermath of the destruction of branch lines brought about by the 'Beeching Report'. The Swanage branch was well covered in it and I was asked to make a few observations during an interview which was filmed at the station, while I was sitting on the foot framing of the 'M7' No. 30053.

Another event that I was very privileged to take part in was the ceremony held on the 'Bluebell Line' on 11th December, 1988 to mark the 40th anniversary of the 'Merchant Navy' class 4-6-2 No. 35027 *Port Line*. As this locomotive was my own engine during its very early days, I was invited to attend as guest of honour. After a short speech, when I toasted No. 35027's next 40 years, I was presented with a bottle of champagne.

After a delightful lunch, Bert Hooker, a former Nine Elms driver, well known for his 1948 interchange trials exploits, and I went up onto the footplate of No. 35027 and took over the controls for one trip; Bert as driver and myself as fireman. She behaved beautifully under Bert's expert hand, and her steaming qualities had not suffered because of her age, although it must be true to say that she is in far better condition now than when steam finished on British Rail.

As I was writing these words, I had a visit from Bill Trite, Chairman of the *Port Line* project, who asked me to sign some photos of No. 35027 in her early days, just as she was when I worked on her. She was photographed on the 'Golden Arrow' boat train and her number plates were obscured, so I asked how he could be sure that it was No. 35027. He pointed out a small but noticeable dent of the fireman's side smoke deflector, telling me he had noted it before on photos of her, but he had to confess that he did not know how it got there.

I cleared up the mystery for him by telling him exactly how it happened. Frank Carter and I were working on the 6.30 pm Waterloo to Bournemouth and Weymouth fast train down during the summer of 1949. We were running at speed through St Denys station on the outskirts of Southampton. A train with a 'T9' at its head was just pulling away from the platform and, as we were about to pass, a pricker, which the fireman had been using to level his fire, appeared over the side of the tender. It struck the smoke deflector of No. 35027 and was wrenched from the fireman's grasp, but landed safely on the coal at the back of the 'T9's' tender leaving the fireman shocked but, fortunately, uninjured.

The damage to our engine was only slight and, therefore, no remedial action was taken but, apparently, it had not escaped the notice of railway enthusiasts and the dent remained there until *Port Line* was rebuilt. I had given the matter no thought since it happened but Bill's remarks brought the incident immediately back to mind.

The year 1990 brought us another GWR locomotive, 0-6-2 tank No. 5619, formerly used in South Wales on coal trains. It packs plenty of power and more than adequately deals with the tasks that are set it at Swanage.

I was working on her with Peter Sykes as my fireman when it occurred to me to set about making up the fire as I used to. With hand picked coal, I started to make up the fire until I had a good bed then allowed it to burn up before adding more until I was satisfied with my efforts. I hasten to add that this was not because I had any doubts about Pete's ability, as he is an excellent fireman, but just to convince myself that I still knew how.

As we left Swanage, I suggested to Pete that he kept the fire just as I had built it. He looked at the fire that was now really hot, picked up the shovel and added coal evenly around the firebox with a steady easy swing. No. 5619 responded to his efforts by quickly moving over to full pressure then just as she was about to 'blow off' Peter put on his injector, cutting it fine, but the needle held steady. No. 5619 responded well to Pete's firing all day, with the last trip, an extra one to bring back a special of empty coaches from Harman's Cross, just as good as the first.

I am a firm believer in having a good fire all the time we are in service, providing it is properly controlled so as to avoid smoke and excess steam, and cannot agree with some who think that keeping a low fire saves coal. Keeping a fire low is not conducive to good steaming and is injurious to tubes and tubeplate. The habit of some fireman of fully closing the dampers on a hot fire on arrival at Harman's Cross is the main reason why we are having problems with fire bars burning. It is true to say that coal is at times to blame for some problems but this can be minimised by using pebbles, broken firebrick or chalk

on the firebars when preparing the fire at the commencement of a day's work.
The extra effort that goes into making up a good fire has its own rewards.
Using hand picked coal is the method that the *Handbook for Railway Steam
Locomotive Enginemen* recommends and long experience has shown me that this
is undoubtedly the best way.

As 1990 was the 50th Anniversary of the 'Battle of Britain' it was decided to
hold a 1940s week-end on the 22nd and 23rd September. On the Sunday I was
at the controls of the 'N7' No. 69621 but for that day she had been re-numbered
and re-lettered 'LNER' to confirm her wartime role.

My fireman was Roger Sinar and we left the engine shed early to couple onto
a goods train loaded with military vehicles for the purpose of having a
photographic record made of the day.

The station had been transformed back to 1940 and sandbags had been placed
around strategic points which were guarded by members of the Home Guard.
War time posters were in evidence everywhere and the station approach road
was filled with jeeps, lorries, Bren gun carriers and a host of other Army
vehicles. The platform was crowded with soldiers, sailors, airmen, nurses, air
raid wardens, fireman and representatives of most other civilian services that
were active during the war.

The group of service men and women gathered around the engine for photos,
and amongst their numbers were two men and a woman dressed in American
uniforms. The photographer, Andrew Wright, was not satisfied with their
appearance, as it worried him that the 'Americans' looked too smart. He asked
them to loll about a bit, and make themselves look more like 'Yanks'. They
obliged by doing just that and to Andrew's delight, one lit up a fat cigar and
then the session began. With the photographing over, we uncoupled from the
train and our first passenger train was pulled into the station.

Passengers, many of them carrying gas masks, joined the train, and we set
back onto it for our first trip to Harman's Cross.

The guard, wearing a tin hat and having a gas mask haversack slung over his
shoulder, gave me the load and in a few minutes we were away.

When we arrived back at Swanage we were greeted with an urgent
announcement that our next train had been cancelled. I must confess that it was
a mystery to me why this was so. After a few minutes a second message
boomed out over the loud speaker system. 'The train standing at this platform
will now form an Evacuation Special. It is not for use by the general public.
There will be a slight delay to this service whilst we await the arrival of
evacuees'.

The evacuees were, in fact, children, many of them disabled, brought to
Swanage by a fleet of taxis whose drivers had conveyed them free of charge so
that they could have a ride beind a steam locomotive. This was something that
most of them had never done before. Soon the station was filled with the
clamour of young voices, as the taxis unloaded their young passengers, and our
train was quickly filled to capacity. Most of the evacuees had labels attached to
their clothing, showing clearly their names and addresses. Many carried gas
mask boxes and little bundles of clothing to add an air of authenticity.

My mind went back over the years to recall many such train loads, but the difference was that those of 50 years ago had no gaiety in their voices and many had tear-stained faces with a look of despair about them. During the day I was constantly reminded of the things that happened during those dark days way back in the 'forties', some good, and some bad. I met several of my old 'mates', some, in fact, that I did not recognise but they all seemed to know me, perhaps because I was doing what they had always associated me with, whereas they had taken other employment and, of course, the passage of time does alter some people more than others. I must admit that I have a poor memory for names, but, strangely, I have an enormous ability to remember numbers.

After 'Battle of Britain' class 4-6-2 No. 34072 *257 Squadron* had taken part in the 'Battle of Britain' 50th anniversary celebrations at Folkestone she was taken to the 'Bluebell Railway' for what was a running in period before she was scheduled to come to Swanage in November 1990.

To give some of the drivers and fireman at Swanage the opportunity to familiarise themselves with the controls of this locomotive, they were kindly invited up to Sheffield Park in October 1990. Although I worked on this class of locomotive for many years, and had probably covered a distance of half a million miles on them, I was also invited for what was regarded as a refresher course. On arrival we were greeted and given a guided tour of No. 34072 by her driver and fireman.

Over 23 years had elapsed since I had driven one of these locomotives, but I quickly realised that I had forgotten nothing, and was immediately at home on the footplate. I was able to take our men around the engine pointing out the features such as oil cups, steam and vacuum brakes, sanding and reversing gears. Some time was spent making sure that every one was acquainted with all the cab fittings and the need to use them in the correct manner. Steam cocks on these locomotives should never be forced shut because, if they are, difficulty will be experienced when they are re-opened, very often calling for a tool to free them which could result in costly damage. The injectors for example only need to be opened a very small amount on both steam and water cocks to get them working correctly, as I had learnt many years ago. Too much of either and they will just not work. Their only vice is a tendency to slip which is easily controlled if a little care is exercised.

A train had been arranged for us to work, thus giving everyone a chance to try their hand at this locomotive, which was by far the biggest that most of them had worked on.

We were well looked after by all at the 'Bluebell Railway' and it was a delight to me at the end of the day to be invited to the 'Drivers Cabin' for a cup of tea and to meet the locomotive crews there. I met Clive Groom at the door and after a cheery greeting, then a handshake, we had a good old chin wag about our days on British Rail, his steam locomotive courses and his associations with the Swanage Railway.

After having tea it was time to leave on our journey back to Bournemouth, so we bade them farewell, expressing the hope that they would pay us a visit at their earliest opportunity. Such moments are tinged with a little sadness but they are the kind of events that are printed indelibly on one's mind, never to be forgotten.

On Saturday 10th November, we had a special day at Swanage to mark the arrival of No. 34072 *257 Squadron* recently beautifully restored at Swindon.

I was the driver and my fireman was Roger Sinar. Roger, a former British Rail fireman, has an easy style of firing to the highest standards which is so like my own that, from the first time that I had him as a mate, I had complete confidence in him making my job so much easier and enjoyable, with no anxious moments to mar the day's work. We signed on at 8.00 am and, after reading the notices, our roster for the day, then the repair book, we set about our preparation duties, carefully checking the state of the boiler, firebox and the fire, which had been lit up for us. After oiling the locomotive I checked that we had sufficient coal and water to complete our duty, and tested the brake and the sanding gear.

We set back into the station to halt alongside a small stage that had been set up for a ceremony to mark the return of one of this class to Swanage after an absence of over 23 years. As soon as we stopped we were surrounded by a large crowd of enthusiasts and I was inundated with questions about my own experiences with this class.

I was introduced to Air Commodore Peter Brothers, CBE, DSO, DFC & Bar and several high-ranking officers of the Royal Air Force, including pilots who had flown with 257 Squadron during the Battle of Britain. The footplate was soon filled with those anxious to have a look at the cab and its controls. Amongst these was Ron Pocklington who had worked on O.V.S. Bulleid's design team and we had a good conversation about the designer and his locomotives which, to my mind, were, in the case of the 'Merchant Navy', 'West Country' and 'Battle of Britain' classes, excellent in every way as anyone who has worked on them will confirm.

A few speeches were made to mark this occasion but very soon it was time for us to move out of the platform to allow our train to be shunted back into it. I asked the Air Commodore if he would be riding in the train or would like to stay on the footplate for the trip up to Harman's Cross. He quickly replied, 'I'll ride with you if I may. I've never had a footplate ride'. To comply with the rules I cleared the cab of all but one other, who was Harry Frith, the well known fitter from Eastleigh Works where the Bullied locos were built.

The Air Commodore had been invited to drive *257 Squadron* out of the station into the siding. I gave him a quick run down of the controls, stressing the need for blowing the whistle before moving to warn the gathering enthusiasts, then, on a tip from the station foreman the Air Commodore blew the whistle and cautiously opened the regulator, moving slowly along the platform, then applying the brake when we were clear of the points. 'That was terrific!' he exclaimed, 'I really enjoyed that!'

Our train was shunted back into the station and I set back onto it in readiness for our first train. Roger coupled onto the coaches while I watched, not, I hasten to add, because I did not trust him to do it properly, but simply because it is my job to do so. The waiting passengers quickly joined the train we were on our way. The locomotive gave a slight slip, so I closed the regulator, waiting for a moment for the slip to stop, then re-opened it giving slight pressure on the locomotive steam brake to prevent a reccurrence and this time we were away. We had started on a low fire which Roger had kept that way in order to keep

BR Standard class '4' 2-6-4T No. 80138 leaves Swanage with the 12.25 pm train to Wareham, 31st August, 1966. These locomotives replaced the ex-LSWR 'M7' class on this service. As these engine were not 'push-pull' fitted the engine would have had to run round its train.

Roy Panting

'Battle of Britain' class 4-6-2 No. 34060 *25 Squadron* minus its smokebox door number plate and nameplates stands in No. 2 platform at Weymouth on 5th July, 1967, just five days before being withdrawn from service. *Colin Stone*

'West Country' class 4-6-2 No. 34001 *Exeter* is seen here at Weymouth, having just arrived with the 3.01 pm from Bournemouth on the 5th July, 1967. By this time the locomotive's numberplate and nameplates had been removed.   *Colin Stone*

A view from the west end of Parkstone station with up and down trains passing. Both trains are made up of a locomotive and 4TC set, and show the sets in their original all-blue livery.
                                                                                                                            Colin Stone

Class '73' electro-diesels Nos. E6021 and E6007 are seen about to leave Bournemouth Central station on the 11.10 am to Waterloo, 19th August, 1967. *Roy Panting*

Birmingham RC&W Co. type '3' Bo-Bo class '33/1' No. 33107 is seen shunting clay wagons at Furzebrook on 15th September, 1981. To the left are the sidings used for oil traffic with a rake of tank wagons in view. *Colin Stone*

A 4-Rep unit is seen at Brockenhurst station in 1987. *Author*

BR diesel electric 0-6-0 shunter No. 09026 is seen on shunting duty at Hamworthy quay during 1987. *Author*

Class '73' electro-diesel No. 73110 about to leave Bournemouth carriage sidings with empty stock, summer 1987. *Author*

Birmingham RC&W Co. type '3' Bo-Bo class '33' is seen at Parkstone station with a 4TC set on a train bound for Bournemouth. A cement mixer had been placed on the down line by vandals and was subsequently struck by a train. The resulting damage to the track can be seen in the distance. *Author*

Ex-LSWR 'T9' class 4-4-0 No. 120 with the author at the controls is seen on the Swanage Railway between Herston and Harman's Cross. *Terry England*

Former Somerset & Dorset driver Johnny Walker is with the author on the footplate of GWR '57XX' class 0-6-0PT No. 7752 at Swanage, whilst Roger Sinar takes water. Johnny Walker was the driver of the last BR steam-hauled passenger train on the Swanage branch, as well as the driver of the final BR passenger train on 1st January, 1972. *Author*

Ivatt '2MT' class 2-6-0 No. 46443 at Swanage. Leaning out of the cab waiting for the guard's 'Right Away'. *Author*

Ex-MR Johnson '1F' class 0-6-0T stands at Harman's Cross station during the 'Gala Weekend' in the summer of 1994. *Author*

Looking out of the cab window of ex-LNER class 'A3' No. 60103 *Flying Scotsman* standing at Swanage station, 16th July, 1994.

Author

the boiler under control, but now, with a few shovelfuls of coal placed expertly around the firebox 257 *Squadron* responded immediately with the steam pressure rising steadily over to the 250 lb. mark. Harry Frith was standing behind me and kept a close watch on the reversing lever to make sure that it held steadily in the position that I had placed it, but he need not have worried because it did not move at all.

The healthy sounding beats of the exhaust were music to the ears, the even rhythm being a testimony to the magnificent work put into the reconstruction, a job really well done. Roger fired up with a few more well placed shovelfuls of coal then closed the firedoor hole. I looked across at him and said 'How do you like her?' His reply was just one word,'Magic!' accompanied by a 'thumbs up' sign that told it all. Despite the 23 year gap since I had been at the controls of one of this class I felt just as much at home as if it had been yesterday, absolutely relaxed and enjoying every minute of it.

The locomotive made light work of the steady incline, and as we approached Harman's Cross station I acknowledged the waves of the crowd lining the road bridge there with a blast on the whistle, which brought forth a cheer as we passed under it. We rolled steadily into the station coming to a smooth halt and Roger climbed smartly down the offside to uncouple, but even before he had touched the ground we were again besieged by a crowd, all anxious to have a closer look at No. 34072. A close watch has to be kept on the enthusiasts because, as much as we love to have them, there are some who do expose themselves to danger in pursuit of photographs, thus causing a headache to engine crews.

Plenty of time was allowed at Harman's Cross and the television team from TVS were on hand to ask the Air Commodore what he had thought of the journey. He replied, 'This is terrific. It is a wonderful memory both for this locomotive and the Squadron'. He then turned to me saying, 'This is super, I cannot remember when I enjoyed myself more'. He shook my hand, then took his leave to make his way for the TV crew who were to film throughout our journey back to Swanage. As we left Harman's Cross it started to rain heavily and, because there were so many photographers along the line, I had to lean out of the cab in order to see. As the camera was focused on me it must have amused the cameraman to see the rain streaming down my face and dripping off my chin. Unpleasant as it was for me, I just had to keep a sharp lookout in case someone thought that the best position for a photograph was in the middle of the track!

We had Ron Pocklington on the footplate with us on our next trip. He was very impressed with the performance of No. 34072 and highly praised the way she has been so lovingly restored.

We had three booked trips that day but it was necessary to run an extra trip which we were delighted to do. On our third trip we had the pleasure of Bert Hooker's company on the footplate. After a handshake and a few friendly words, Bert asked, 'Do you mind if I do the firing?' I replied, 'I am sure Roger will be agreeable to that, then added, 'That is if you can keep pace with me!' with a broad grin on my face. I have known Bert for many years but never before had he been my fireman, although I have fired for him on No. 35027 whilst on the 'Bluebell'. It goes without saying that Bert had not the slightest difficulty in making No. 34072 steam, and in a manner that would have made men half his age feel that they were in the company of a master.

During the 1990 Christmas period we took delivery of two locomotives, one, an 0-6-0 USA tank loco to be used here after some work is done, and the other, a 'T9' 4-4-0 No. 120, is on loan for a period from the National Railway Museum York.

Being a driver at Swanage has meant that the number of locomotives I have worked on has steadily increased and on being told that the former LNER 0-6-0T No. 69023 'J72' now named *Joem* was expected at Swanage I realised that this would be my 100th class.

I casually informed Andrew Wright of this fact but he made little comment, however he must of made a mental note of it as events were to show. A few days later I was booked on with No. 69023 resplendent in her LNER light green beautifully cleaned and polished by several cleaners.

As we approached the platform I was surprised to see a large crowd gathered and a television camera in position by our train. I wondered what the event could be and much to my amazement I was greeted by David Cash who presented me with a beautifully engraved plaque to commemorate my 100th class of locomotive bearing the following inscription:

Stan Symes
Congratulations On Your 100th
Class Of Locomotive
From All Your Friends And
Colleagues On The Swanage Line
December 8th 1991

I was also presented with a large framed photograph of me on the footplate of No. 69023 on the day she arrived in Swanage. Margaret Clark of the catering department had baked a very large fruit cake and iced it with the words, CONGRATULATIONS ON YOUR 100TH.

I felt elated by their kindness and undaunted in the event that anyone should think it was a birthday cake. The same evening this little ceremony was shown on TV and made a nice end to the day for me. Needless to say the plaque will be treasured by me for the rest of my days.

On Friday 19th March, 1993, a charter train was run for a group of photographers of the railway press and it was headed by two Bulleid 'Pacifics' coupled together for the first time since the end of steam on British Rail. The engines were 'West Country' class No. 34105 *Swanage* on loan from the Watercress Line, and our own 'Battle of Britain' class No. 34072 *257 Squadron*. The driver on *Swanage* was Roger Sinar and his fireman was Paul McDonald whilst I was the driver and Mike Standhaft my fireman on *257 Squadron*. We were hauling a train of 8 coaches plus a large van.

We were at the disposal of the photographers and when they had all boarded we worked the train to Harman's Cross. Our passengers left the train and made their way down the track selecting vantage points from which to take photographs, then when they were in safe positions we propelled the train back down the line stopping just short of the crossing at Quar Farm. At a given signal we worked the train up to Harman's Cross putting on a display of smoke and steam guaranteed to satisfy the most discerning cameraman.

This procedure was repeated four times, then the photographers rejoined the train at Harman's Cross station. Both locomotives ran-round the train and we hauled it back to Swanage. On arrival there the order of the locomotives was reversed, this time with No. 34072 leading.

The weather on this day could not have been better, it was brilliantly sunny but just enough chill in the air to show up the exhaust steam from our chimneys to full advantage and the coal gave off a good amount of smoke, which when fired up at the right moment produced a dramatic effect. The crews were all former British Rail footplate men with over 100 years of experience, I alone having 55 years to my credit.

Leaving Swanage with the second stage of our charter train we were requested to stop at a point ¾ of a mile beyond Herston station, here the passengers alighted and set up their cameras at various points, some on embankments, some on step ladders, and some even on lineside trees.

We set back into Herston, then when given the 'off' took the train away at a brisk pace to give the best possible effect in our run past. A video produced by Classic Video entitled *Swanage at Swanage, A day to remember*, has captured this scene to perfection and is well worth watching.

After five such runs we picked up the photographers and made our way up to Harman's Cross, then back at a leisurely pace to Swanage.

No. 34105 *Swanage* made more runs but our 'M7' tank was coupled to the front of it and a further session of photos took place. It was a good day for all the photographers and crews alike and a series of wonderful photos appeared in several railway magazines as a result of it.

Since working on my 100th class of loco I have driven the Yugoslavian built 'Yankee' 0-6-0 tank, the class '25' diesel electric, 'Thomas the Tank' 0-6-0 loco, and the class '108' 2-Car dmu, giving a grand total of 104 types to date.

Early in 1994 I heard a rumour that the LNER 'A3' class 4-6-2 No. 60103 *Flying Scotsman* was coming to Swanage but treated this as a joke because its axle weight was heavier than anything that had ever run over this line. However the rumours proved to be true and after an eventful journey by road from the Nene Valley Railway, near Peterborough, the engine arrived at midday on 15th July, and was off-loaded.

The engine and tender, which had arrived earlier in the week, were re-united and the boiler was filled with water, then the tender also. After being coaled up, the fire was lit at midnight to raise steam.

To my delight I was booked to work the first passenger train, leaving at 10.30 am on Saturday 16th July, and I signed on duty at 8.00 am expecting to have to prepare the locomotive, but I was greeted with a scene of feverish activity as she was being prepared by Roland Kennington, who is the engineer in charge of *Flying Scotsman*, and driver Nigel Clark.

Roland showed me round the locomotive, pointing out the oiling positions and advising me as to the correct lubricants to use. He also gave me a rundown on the positions of various cocks, levers, and gauges.

He took the locomotive out of the depot and a light engine test run was made to make sure that all platforms, bridges, and structures had sufficient clearance. A second trip was made this time hauling the empty train that was standing in the platform in readiness for the 10.30 am.

No difficulties were encountered on either trip and on arrival back at Swanage I climbed on to the footplate in readiness for our first passenger service.

The station was filled with enthusiasts wanting to get a closer look at the *Flying Scotsman* so when I received the guard's signal to start I gave a good blast on the whistle as a warning, made sure everyone was clear, then gently but firmly opened the regulator. She responded instantly and pulled steadily out of the station, with no sign of a slip, but with crisp sounding exhaust beats that brought joy to my heart.

I pulled up the reversing lever, perhaps a little too much as I detected a slight retarding effect, but half a turn more on the reverser corrected this and the exhaust beats evened out.

After passing the end of the 10 mph speed restriction I gave her a touch more on the regulator and she smoothly gathered speed and I got an immediate feel of her immense power.

Running into Herston station I made allowance for the extra length of the tender and asked Roland if I had stopped at the correct point as the platform was on the opposite side of the engine. 'Perfect', he replied.

I must say that I was impressed by the ease that No. 60103 pulled away from Herston and gathered speed in a fashion worthy of this thoroughbred. The station at Harman's Cross is a steady upward climb from Herston but the *Flying Scotsman* took it in her stride, well within the time allowed, I may add.

We ran-round the train at Harman's Cross, making a brief stop for a welcome cup of tea, then we were soon on our way back to Swanage. With the short platform at Herston it is essential to stop correctly with the last 2 coaches at the platform and brought the train to a halt on the fireman's tip. To make sure that for the rest of the day I stopped in the same spot I dropped a knob of coal down on to the track as a marker. On arrival back at Swanage Roland said, 'I will leave you to it, you obviously don't need me, so I will see you later'.

We had just started a new system at Swanage whereby every driver working on a class of locomotive he is not familiar with must receive instructions and must be accompanied by a qualified driver, or the owner's representative.

I asked Roland, 'Would you sign my paper for me?', but he laughed and said, 'You must be joking'. I asked him again when he joined us on our 4th trip and explained its purpose; this time he said, 'Of course I will sign it' which he did, and after thanking him I folded it and slipped it in my pocket without looking at it.

At my invitation Roland worked the 4th trip up to Harman's Cross with me acting as conductor as he is not familiar with the line. Needless to say he worked it to perfection as he has worked this locomotive over many miles in this country , as well as the USA and Australia.

On leaving the footplate I thanked Roland warmly for his advice and help, then shook his hand in gratitude for a memorable and trouble free day. When I arrived at home that evening I looked at the form he had signed earlier and under the heading 'Instructors Remarks' he had written, 'Who am I to teach this Gentleman?', which I thought was very nice of him.

The 28th August, 1994 marked my 55 years on the footplate and happily I was again booked to work on *Flying Scotsman*, with Bob Budden as my fireman. I have always made a point of being punctual and this day was no exception.

I boarded the *Flying Scotsman*, had a few friendly words to say to Bob, then made the usual preparation checks.

A call from the engine cleaner that a cup of tea was ready was timed to perfection as I had just filled the cylinder lubricator with steam oil thus completing my preparation of the locomotive.

I enjoyed a leisurely drink, then went to move No. 60103 forward for coal. This was a signal for a burst of activity with many hands making light work of filling the tender with enough coal for a good day's train running.

Our train was not made-up until 10.25 am. We went out to our train and Bob quickly coupled on, then after a brake test we left five minutes late.

I pulled away as briskly as the speed restriction would allow then having cleared it gave No. 60103 full regulator thus rapidly bringing our speed up to maximum for the line.

Bob was steadily firing, with the steam pressure gauge almost over to the red line, and it is true to say that his management of the boiler was superb all day as he rarely let her blow off at the safety valves, and kept smoke down to the minimum.

On arrival at Harman's Cross we were only one minute late having made up four on the journey.

After arriving back at Swanage I was pleasantly surprised to hear an announcement over the Tannoy system, 'Congratulations to the Driver, Stan Symes on completion of 55 years on the footplate, in recognition of which we are happy to make him a presentation and express the hope that he will continue to do so for many more years'. I was duly presented with a good bottle of Sherry to celebrate at home, not on duty, I hasten to add.

I appreciate such acts of kindness and friendship which are the very essence of the Swanage Railway. I love every minute of working there.

I thoroughly enjoyed my day's work and was again treated to one more day on the *Flying Scotsman* before her departure. I consider it a privilege to work on such a locomotive and would not have missed it for anything.

Conclusion

I have worked on locomotives for 55 years and although this may not be a record it is a darned good average.

I am now over 72 and as yet I have had no difficulty in passing the medical examination for driving so I will carry on in that capacity for as long as I am able.

Whatever happens in the future no one can take away the joy I have felt in working on all forms of traction, nor the memories of a great breed of men who sadly are no more. I am blessed with the continued friendship of former work mates and colleagues and like nothing better than to talk about our days on steam locomotives.

I am also fortunate in having the friendship of three men in America who share the same interests. One is Captain Frank Dietz of the United States Air Force whom I met by chance on my way to the Model Railway Exhibition in London during the time he was stationed in this country at Bentwaters Air Base. He has helped me in many ways to further my interest in US railroad modelling, sending me books, plans and equipment for which I am truly grateful. The second is Phil Trainor, a resident of Bellaire, Texas, who has sent me Railroad Rule books, timetables, and lots of information on the Santa Fe Railroad, which, along with the Union Pacific, I have a great interest in. I appreciate his efforts on my behalf, and although we have never met, I count him as a true friend.

The last but not least is Carl F. LeMier Snr who I have been corresponding with for something approaching 40 years. He has sent books, magazines, model railroad equipment, badges, calendars, holiday information, maps, and countless other items.

We met for the first time at his home in Salinas, California during May 1993 and we had several outings together to San Francisco, San Jose, Monterey and one day he took us to the California State Railroad Museum in Sacramento, a round trip of over 400 miles, which he said was just around the corner.

He is a great character with a distinguished war record and has a string of medals including the Silver Star, three Bronze Stars, three Purple Hearts awarded for being wounded in action, the Criox De Guerre with palm leaf, and many more medals for action in North Africa, Italy, France and Germany. He has been a truck driver, covering more than 5,000,000 miles, a Security Guard for Wells Fargo, and now at 76 he makes excellent wooden toys including trucks (lorries), cars, trains, and planes, all beautifully finished and a credit to him.

May our friendship continue for many more years.

My sincere thanks go to Graham Mimms who encouraged me to write this book, insisting that I should do so, in the hope that it would enlighten others as to the joys of working on all forms of locomotives.

Appendix One

Motive Power

During the past 55 years I have worked on a wide variety of locomotives and electric multiple units and my own opinion of these may not be shared by all who have also fired and driven them.

The main feature I remember with the first locomotive that I ever fired, namely the 0-6-0 'G6' class No. 239, was the handbrake which was the only brake fitted and this was used by the fireman. Built for shunting, these locos were strong and good steamers but at the end of a busy day constantly applying and releasing the handbrake, the fireman was not sorry when his relief arrived.

Adams 'T1' Class 0-4-4T

Small and compact, they made good shunting locomotives and were fitted with a steam brake, generally used by the fireman or by the driver in conjunction with the vacuum brake. The injectors were prone to suddenly blow out if the brake was applied when setting back, much to the annoyance of the shunter.

Adams 'B4' Class 0-4-0T

These little engines were used for shunting, dock work and light, short distance freight trains and were surprisingly strong but, again, only fitted with a handbrake, they kept the fireman busy. Despite the cramped footplate and very small coal bunkers, which were difficult to get at, I enjoyed working on them. Making the fire up at the start of a turn, using hand picked coal made for easier work as a good box of fire would last for a long time but the injectors had to be opened carefully and had the same tendency as the 'T1' class to blow out when shunting. I never ceased to be amazed at the capabilities of these incredible locomotives.

Adams 'A12' Class 0-4-2 'Jubilees'

They were small but, providing a good head of steam was kept, could be made to perform well and it was always a challenge when working on these locomotives to keep the steam gauge right over to the blowing off point. I am happy to be able to say that I always managed it and although this class were withdrawn early in my career, I have a soft spot for good old No. 612.

Adams 'T3' Class 4-4-0 'Highflyers'

My first regular driver taught me the basic principles of firing on this class of locomotive and, as a result, I always think back to those happy days. With large driving wheels they were originally built for express passenger work and they had a good turn of speed but, as larger engines came on the scene, they were relegated to local passenger and light freight work. They had a roomy but rather open cab which afforded little protection when running tender first, but were never a problem to make steam and I enjoyed working on them.

Drummond 'K10' Class 4-4-0 'Small Hoppers'

These were real maids of all work during the war years, often being called on to do work which should have been done by larger locomotives. They had roomy cabs with good wide seat boxes and a tender that was easy to get at. The low front of the tender made for easy fire cleaning and they were well liked by most men that worked on them.

Drummond 'L11' Class 4-4-0 'Large Hoppers'
Slightly larger than the 'K10', but, of exactly the same tractive effort. Although having larger tenders than the 'K10' they were so alike that to all intents and purposes they were the same.

Drummond 'L12' Class 4-4-0 'Bulldogs'
With slightly less power than the 'K10s' and 'L11s', they were, however, more suited to faster passenger work on account of their 6 ft 7 in. driving wheels. The cab layout of these three classes were very similar but the 'L12' had a stepped down floor which made them awkward for fire cleaning. Used mostly on local passenger work and often expected to pull long trains, they were hard work for the fireman and in consequence were not so well liked.

Drummond '700' Class 0-6-0 'Black Motors'
Widely used on all classes of freight trains for shunting and also passenger trains, such as workmen's specials, they did sterling work for over 50 years and were a credit to their designer, Dugald Drummond. Not built for comfort, they had narrow uncomfortable seats in keeping with Drummond's belief that a driver could not do his work sitting down! They were narrow and the cab was very open making tender first running a misery in winter.

Drummond 'T9' Class 4-4-0 'Greyhounds'
Well liked by all, they lived up to their nickname as they were capable of speeds up to the maximum permitted speed of 85 mph for steam trains on the Southern, as Bournemouth men can testify when working the 'Airways' trains between Bournemouth West and Victoria, running non stop between Christchurch and the London terminus. They were inclined to slip in adverse weather but, skilful handling could eliminate this. Often used on freight trains in their final years they would put up a creditable performance, but care in braking with loose coupled trains was essential.

Drummond 'M7' Class 0-4-4T
Another firm favourite of mine, because on reaching the Push and Pull Link at Bournemouth we had one allocated to us and worked on it most of the time. Ideally suited to this work they were good steaming engines, compact yet having a roomy comfortable cab. They were kept in spotless condition with friendly competition for the best footplate. No. 106 was my last 'M7' and she was one of the best, easily covering the trip from Bournemouth West to Brockenhurst without the need to take water even when hauling as many as eight coaches.

Drummond 'D15' Class 4-4-0
These larger Drummond locomotives had several advantages over the 'K10', 'L12' and 'L11' classes and were ideal for passenger work, having a bigger firebox and a boiler which was superheated. Their free steaming qualities made them popular, especially with Eastleigh men who had a link whose work was centred around them. This 'D15' Link worked trains to Bournemouth, Salisbury, Portsmouth etc., and as they were allocated individual locomotives, they took great pride in them, keeping cabs and tools in excellent condition. They were probably the best 4-4-0s that Drummond built and were eventually replaced by BR Standard class '4' 76000 series locos.

Drummond 'T14' Class 'Paddleboats'
These often re-designed locomotives were never up to the tasks that were set them and were not at all popular with engine crews. Tall firemen were better suited for these

engines with their high set steam control wheels and low stoke hole of a footplate, difficult to fire to firegrate, calling for a long reach and a hefty swing of the shovel. Although they had four cylinders they were a poor substitute for a 'King Arthur' or a 'Nelson' and no tears were shed when they were withdrawn from service. I had several trips to London on them and never had a bad trip for steam, but I hated cleaning the fire which was very difficult even if you were well built.

Urie and Maunsell 'H15', 'S15' and 'H16' Classes 4-6-0 and 4-6-2T

These were excellent freight locomotives and did sterling work throughout their working lives. They were well liked by all crews in that capacity but, when pressed into passenger work were rough riding at speed making it difficult to keep the dust down. They had large comfortable cabs, making fire cleaning easy and all controls were easy to reach. They were never difficult to make steam and they had a good look out. My favourite of these classes was 'H15' No. 521, a Bournemouth engine so free steaming that she would make steam with a candle in the firebox!

Urie and Maunsell 'N15' 'King Arthur' Class 4-6-0

This class consisted of 74 locomotives in three groups the 'Eastleigh', 'Urie' and 'Scotch' Arthurs with the 'Urie' group being slightly less powerful and having 180 lb. pressure instead of the 200 lb. pressure of the rest. All of them were good to work on but I preferred the 'Scotch' 'Arthurs' with their larger rounded top cabs, and have spent many a happy hour on them, especially on the run down from Bournemouth to Oxford. Various engines in this class were modified by fitting multiple blast pipes and larger chimneys and alterations to valves and pistons were also carried out. No. 755 was a fine example and was the pick of the bunch.

'N15X' 'Remembrance' Class 4-6-0 Rebuilt by Maunsell

Although these engines were very close to the 'Arthurs' in tractive effort, they were never regarded as being in the same class by the men who worked on them. Difficult to fire to and slow to get going on account of their larger driving wheels, they did, however, have a good turn of speed if not hauling too heavy a train. I liked the easily operated injectors fitted and the challenge that they presented to the fireman, but I was glad that none of this class were allocated to Bournemouth and we only worked on them when they were used on Summer time excursions or relief trains.

On one such occasion, in company with driver Jack Atfield we worked a train of 14 coaches to London, the day being Good Friday and the locomotive was No. 2329 *Stephenson*. With this semi-fast train we lost time getting away from stations but on the long run from Basingstoke to Waterloo managed to pull back most of that time with Jack pushing her along at a creditable pace. I had no problems in making her steam but with this load I was shovelling constantly most of the way. We ran into No 10 platform at Waterloo, where we had relief, only to be informed that this train formed our 1.30 pm back. We walked the length of the train only to find another of the same class backing onto the coaches, this time it was No. 2331 *Beattie*.

Our first stop was at Woking and No. 2331 made hard work of the climb to Pirbright Junction despite the fact that Jack was using full regulator and 45 per cent cut off, and the fact that she was right over on the 180 lb. blowing off point. With a similar hard slog out of Basingstoke up to Litchfield tunnel, we were losing time through no fault of our own. Once through the tunnel she picked up speed rapidly and we held our own right down to Brockenhurst.

Sway and Pokesdown banks proved formidable obstacles resulting in more loss of time. We arrived at the mess room lobby after relief at Bournemouth Central dusty and tired, only to be met by the office clerk who was at the window, telephone in hand saying,

'Control are on the phone and want to know why you lost time with the 1.30 down?' At this Jack saw red and exclaimed, 'Let me have the phone and I'll tell them, in no uncertain terms, exactly why we lost time with the 'Remembrance'. What the hell do they expect with a train of 14 coaches?' The Clerk, fearing Jack's reaction on the phone, would not part with it, so had to be content with Jack's retort, 'Tell them they will get my report if and when I get a lost time ticket!' but he never did.

Maunsell 'Schools' 'V' Class 4-4-0

The beautiful clean lines of the 'Schools' class made them, in my opinion, the best looking 4-4-0 ever built. They were Bournemouth depot's main line locomotives when I first started on the Southern Railway and they had a very distinctive appearance. Kept spotlessly clean by the cleaners and looked after with pride by their crews they had a good record for timekeeping and were liked by everyone who worked on them.

They were incredibly easy to fire to. All one had to do was to keep a steeply sloping fire and they would stay right over on the full pressure line with no difficulty whatsoever.

Maunsell 'Lord Nelson' Class 4-6-0

The 'Nelsons' replaced the 'Schools' at Bournemouth when it became evident that a more powerful locomotive was required for express passenger work. These four cylinder locomotives with their long fireboxes called for a completely different way of firing which, when mastered, proved them to be as free in steaming as the 'Schools'.

They were harder to dispose of and young inexperienced firemen found them difficult to manage; but as much as we liked our 'Schools' it must be said that the 'Nelsons' were a whole lot better. My best memory of a trip on a 'Nelson' was on No. 863 *Lord Rodney* when returning from Oxford on our Birkenhead turn.

As we passed through the junction at Didcot, the Great Western 'Red Dragon' was approaching at speed, hauled by a 'Castle', the driver giving us a wave and a short blast on the whistle as he overtook us. My driver, Syd Adams, said, 'Shall we catch him up?' 'Yes, let's!', I replied, so he opened the regulator wide and No. 863 responded at once, so I fired steadily to her until we were almost level with the 'Castle', then sat on my seat with my feet up as we went by with Syd giving a derisory toot as we did so. As soon as we had passed him, the Western driver opened out the 'Castle' and again he overtook us with the fireman shovelling coal as fast as he could. Syd had eased the regulator as we had gained speed, but now over went the lever by one nick and again the regulator swung over to full, so I added more coal to the fire as we gained on the 'Red Dragon'. We slipped by him again and I was sitting down, feet up as we did so, with Syd giving one long and one short on the whistle. The passengers of both trains had sensed the spirit of friendly rivalry and waved as we passed. Not to be outdone, the 'Castle's' driver had, obviously, dropped the lever over more as was indicated by the roar from its chimney accompanied by volumes of smoke and sparks ascending vertically from it.

In all we passed the 'Red Dragon' four times but, as we were fast approaching Reading, we knew that we would have to stop as we had to cross over the up main line on which he was running, so as we slowed down we gave him a cheery wave, with me still sitting down. I never did see the fireman's face, all I saw of his was his backside and his shovel moving rapidly from tender to firebox, almost in time with the flashing piston rods of the 'Castle'. The last time they went by us the 'Red Dragon' was breathing flames from its chimney but the 'Nelson' with its large chimney had made no fuss at all.

Maunsell 'N', 'N1', 'U' and 'U1' Classes 2-6-0

These classes were very similar in appearance and were good all round mixed traffic locomotives, equally at home on either passenger or freight trains. As with the 'Schools' class, all that was needed to make them steam was a good well sloping fire, keeping the back end of the firebox well filled and the front fairly light, taking care not to clog the space under the brick arch with coal. I found that firing to them was almost effortless and that they were clean to work on as the coal was behind lockers and a small access door. They were sure footed with plenty of power, especially the 'N1s' and 'U1s' with 3 cylinders.

Maunsell 'Q' Class 0-6-0

Good for light freight work and shunting but I did not like them on passenger work as they would often buffet about at speed giving the crew a rough ride and shaking the coal forward in the tender. I worked on one as a young fireman, along with a No.1 Link driver who was always very smart in appearance and always wore a stiff white collar. The steam reverser was troublesome and at our first opportunity the driver decided to add oil to the hydraulic cylinder so, telling me to join him, we climbed up on to the foot framings, taking with us spanners and the necessary oil.

Before leaving the footplate he said, 'These locos are different to an "M7" and it is best to place the lever in the mid position; it is much easier to fill them that way'. He carried out this operation leaving the operating handle in the locked position. He removed the filling plug and slowly poured the oil down the pipe, taking care not to get an airlock. Just as the oil level in the cylinder reached the full mark, the reverser moved smartly back into reverse forcibly ejecting the oil and the driver, who was right in the line of fire, was smothered in oil. He calmly wiped the oil from his overall jacket and stiff collar, then turned to me saying, 'There's just one thing I forgot to mention Stan, always remember to shut the steam off before attempting to fill an hydraulic cylinder!'

Bulleid 'Q1' Class 0-6-0

The 'Q1s', Austerity locomotives, were just what the name implies, because they had just the bare essentials to make what was a very efficient locomotive, but they were strange, having no running plates or wheel splashers and a boiler casing shaped like half of a luncheon meat tin, hence the nickname 'spam cans'. The small front plated area around the smokebox provided a precarious perch for cleaning out the ash and often a plank was placed across the buffers in the interest of safety when carrying out this task.

They were ugly but excellent engines and were far superior to the 'Qs', having a large firebox and boiler, making them free steaming. The closed in cab provided good protection from the elements, but the large hydrostatic lubricator fitted on the fireman's side of the cab caused many a headache as they were too close to the side window and great care had to be taken not to give yourself a nasty blow on the side of your head.

The very first time I worked on one we were asked to run a special freight train from Eastleigh Yard to Marchwood on the Fawley branch. Bournemouth men did not know the branch line so it was necessary to have a conductor to show us the route. On returning, tender first, I placed the leather pouch containing the tablet for the single line on the arm provided at Totton and, as I turned back into the cab, my side gauge glass literally exploded with a force that shattered all three of the armour glass protectors, also bending the perforated back plate like a horseshoe. The flying glass cut me across the nose but the restrictor valve did its work well and I was able to close the gauge cocks without difficulty. The cut was not serious but the incident was alarming, probably caused by the high boiler pressure of these engines. I have had several gauge glasses break, but never one like that. These locomotives were often used on passenger trains and, despite their small wheels, would give a very creditable performance.

Bulleid 'Merchant Navy' Class 4-6-2

O.V.S. Bulleid has come in for a fair amount of criticism but to the men who have worked on these locomotives he is highly regarded. Without hesitation I can affirm that these are the finest locomotives on which I have been privileged to work. Their only vice was the small windows originally fitted but these were greatly enlarged and angled later, giving an infinitely better look out. They must have been one of the most free steaming locomotives ever built and had a turn of speed that, in the right hands, could be achieved very economically. In their original form they would coast for miles with little loss of speed, but this feature was lost when they were re-built and, in my humble opinion, they were far superior when they were as Bulleid built them.

Bulleid 'West Country' and 'Battle of Britain' Class 4-6-2

Smaller and lighter than the 'Merchant Navy' class, they had a much wider route availability allowing them to be used on most lines on the Southern. Most of these locomotives were built without dampers which made them more difficult to control at first until one got used to them. This feature, along with the wheel design and steam operated generator, followed North American practice, as did the rocking grates with which they were fitted.

Again the original front windows were small and almost useless because they were quick to get dirty and impossible to clean on the run. They replaced the 'Merchant Navy' class at Bournemouth in 1950 despite a strong protest from the footplate staff, as we feared that they would be far inferior but we were pleasantly surprised when we received our new 'West Country' class.

The first three were Nos. 34093 *Saunton*, 34094 *Mortehoe*, 34095 *Brentor* and they had wider cabs, rocking and drop grates and larger tenders with a water capacity of 5,500 gallons.

My own engine was No. 34093 and she was a superb example of this class and our very first trip on her showed that we had a wonderful machine in our charge. The drop grate could be operated with one hand and her steaming qualities were such that never at any time did we have any difficulty in maintaining a full head of steam. To be allocated one's own locomotive was a guarantee that they would be well looked after by the two drivers and two firemen, as it was to their benefit to see that all repairs were carried out and that tools and equipment were in tip top order.

So good was No. 34093 that I had plenty of time, even on a London trip, to clean brass, copper and paint on the footplate because it was seldom necessary for me to have to add coal to the fire after Winchester. Driver Syd Futcher and I worked as a team on No. 34093 and every day was a joy to both of us, as I have previously stated, with a sense of achievement at the end of each and every journey.

My next locomotive with driver Frank Horn, No. 34108 *Wincanton* was almost as good as 34093. It was every bit as clean but the newer type rocking grate fitted was not as good as the drop door type for the fireman, so why they were re-designed I will never know!

LB&SC Locomotives

Various types of LB&SC locomotives worked into our area and I have had some experience on the following types but not sufficient to form a firm opinion on them, other than the 'Remembrance' class. The 'Terrier' tank locomotives were good for shunting with an excellent brake, but they had a very small cab and I much preferred the 'G6' class for this type of work.

I only worked on the 'K' class Mogul on one occasion which was an unforgettable day as previously narrated.

The same applies to the 'H1' Brighton Atlantic. It was just a one day event, brought about by the fact that the No. 32038 *Portland Bill* had suffered a hot driving axle box and had been repaired at Bournemouth Loco Dept. She was run in for a few days and it was on a local passenger turn that I spent a day on her, which was enjoyable but did not entail sufficient work to form any conclusion as to the worth of this class.

USA 2-8-0 Class
These locomotives were shipped from the USA to Southampton Docks with the coupling rods and valve gear stored inside their tenders. They were towed to Eastleigh Works where valve gear was fitted, making these powerful locomotives ready for use, when required, in France after the landings in Normandy.

The American style of rocking grate made the cleaning of the fire the work of a few minutes and after taking coal and water, the crew left her ready for the next part of the duty.

These engines were ideal for freight working with their air brakes and tremendous pulling power. The large firebox made them free steamers but the open topped ash pans made them difficult to control. The short reversing lever was also a source of trouble but a length of tubing was often placed over the handle to give more leverage, thus minimising the problem.

GWR Locomotives
I will readily admit that I was not a lover of Great Western locomotives but having said that I would be the first to say that they had some very good points. They were very strong and seldom did they slip. They were free steaming and had a blower that would very nearly lift the firebars out but the very open cabs were a disadvantage in bad weather or when running tender first; certainly not to be compared to the comfort of a 'Merchant Navy's' cab. Neither did they have the superb running qualities of the latter and seemed to want pushing every inch of the way! The low position of the firehole door and the absence of a shovelling plate, coupled with their hungry appetite for coal, meant that the fireman seldom used the small seat provided.

They had an advantage in their degree of standardisation that made working on various types easier, with most controls of a uniform pattern, as opposed to the infinite variety of Southern locomotives.

These words may offend the many GWR enthusiasts but they are my honest opinions.

Many a Southern driver took advantage of the excellent sanding qualities of GW engines and on days when the rail was bad the driver of the 'Royal Wessex' would ask the GW driver of the train that preceded it out of Weymouth to sand the rail between Upwey and Bincombe tunnel. Giving a new sponge cloth to the Western driver and enduring some friendly sarcasm was a small price to pay for the assurance that no problems would be encountered at this trouble spot, because we knew the Western men could be relied upon.

I worked on the following classes of Western locomotives: the 'Halls', 'Granges', 'Panniers', '43XX', '51XX' and, most recently, 0-6-2 tank loco No. 5619 on loan to the Swanage Railway.

Like all GWR locomotives, I found it was covered in oil cups, corks and boxes set in all kinds of weird and wonderful positions calling for a contortionist or a trained monkey to get at some of them, but having successfully located them and and duly filled them with oil I was now ready to see what No. 5619 was capable of.

My fireman was Malcolm Collop and he had been on her once before so was familiar with the controls and I was soon able to clear up one or two points I needed to know.

As soon as we left Swanage on our first trip it was evident, by the way she literally walked the train away, that here we had exceptional pulling power. I found that on pulling the reversing lever up it moved with very little effort and it was not necessary to close the regulator as in the case of the pannier tank No. 7752. This, of course, is on account of the fact that the '56XX' is fitted with piston valves and the 'pannier' has slide valves.

The '56XX' moved along so briskly that I found I could work her in 20 per cent cut off and easily maintain time with only a small amount of regulator opening. She responded well to steady firing and just before she reached the blowing off point Malcolm put on the injector and she held her pressure well against the inflow of water. She was light on water and coal and steamed well all day, making very little ash in the smokebox.

I have had several enjoyable days on her and have experienced no problems whatsoever so, I am beginning to really like this engine which is something I never thought I would say about a GWR engine but, fair is fair!

LNER Locomotives

I have only worked on a few types of LNER locomotivess, the 'V2s', the 'A3' *Flying Scotsman*, the 'A4' *Sir Nigel Gresley*, 'N7' No. 69621 and 'J72' *Joem*.

The 'V2s' were on loan to replace 'West Country' and 'Battle of Britain' locomotives which were, temporarily, withdrawn following an axle failure on the Salisbury to Exeter Line. These 'V2's helped to fill the gap for a few weeks but, although they did the job reasonably well, they could not be compared with the Bulleid Pacifics. I found them pleasant to work on but would not venture to give a firm opinion on them as I had no long runs to be able to assess their capabilities.

The 'A4', of course, was an entirely different 'kettle of fish' and it was obvious from the first touch of the regulator that here was a locomotive that was a master of the job.

The peculiar reversing lever resembling a hand brake was no problem. The bucket seats were a luxury and the rhythm of the three cylinders' exhaust was a delight to the ears.

It was my one regret that we only had a short trip on the 'A4' and I would have liked a trip to London on one to be able to compare it with the 'Merchant Navy' class.

The 'N7' No. 69621 was on loan to Swanage during the summer of 1990 and from the very first time I worked on her I knew that here we had a locomotive that was just right for this line. Free steaming, exceptionally light on coal and water, with a large very comfortable cab having every control within easy reach, plus a good lookout, made her ideal in every way. It is a great pity that there are no more of her class around, because we would love to have one of them.

All credit must go to those who re-built her to such high standards making her a joy to work on.

I liked the Westinghouse air brake because, having worked on the early Southern electrics, I was fully conversant with it and found it easy to operate.

The ease with which she handled trains over the 1 in 76 gradient was impressive and with a fireman like Roger Sinar, who could ask for anything more.

My opinion of LNER locos is very favourable indeed and I would like to work on more if the opportunity presents itself.

LMS Locomotives

Firstly the class '5MT', or 'Black Five', the class that has always been regarded as one of the best classes of British locomotives earning a reputation for free steaming.

A very disturbing incident occurred one day with No. 45493 when I was working the Poole to York train on a Saturday morning. We had 13 coaches from Poole and in consequence I had a banking engine attached to the rear of the train and as we gathered speed along the flat before the bank, I heard a peculiar noise and looking down was horrified to see slivers of wood coming from under the tender. My first instincts were to suspect that the water pick up scoop was in the lowered position, but my fireman, Dougie Robinson, soon allayed my suspicions by demonstrating that the scoop was fully up and secured.

Suddenly the engine rose about 2 ft up into the air, crashing back down on to the rail and the offending noise stopped at once. Not wanting to stop in the worst part of the bank with the banker blasting away in the rear, I decided to run on to Parkstone station where I was booked to stop.

I shut off steam approaching the station and started to apply the brake, but when I did we were completely wreathed in steam and I had difficulty in seeing the end of the platform. Having stopped I fully applied the brake, then closed the vacuum small jet and shut off the steam brake.

I sent Dougie back to tell the guard that I was going to examine the engine and would inform him when I had ascertained the problem. A quick examination showed that the steam brake pull rod pin had come out and the rod had dropped down, thus chipping slivers of wood from the sleepers and at the point where the engine had risen from the track, the rod had struck the tie rod of a pair of trailing points leading across into the gas works and was deflected down under the sleepers. This sent the crank under the steam brake piston crashing through the brake cylinder, completely destroying it, hence the volumes of steam when I had stopped at Parkstone.

As the pull rod was now trailing, no further damage had occurred to the track and it was in a convenient position for me to secure it to the underside of the tender.

Obtaining some sheet ropes from the goods office, I tied the rod tightly to the most accessible point. I was now ready to move and I informed the signalman at Branksome by phone that I would work the train forward to Bournemouth where a replacement engine would be required.We were soon on our way, the whole incident only causing 10 minutes delay to the train.

The 'Black Five' was a firm favourite of mine, handling any train with ease and it is easy to see why the Standard class '5MT' 73000 series locomotive was modelled after them.

'Class 2P' 4-4-0

This was a speedy locomotive, given a sensible load, and was comparable to our own 'T9' class in many respects.

Class '4F' 0-6-0

This was the only LMS locomotive I did not like as they were rough riding when used on passenger work such as on the Somerset and Dorset, which is where I did my work on them as a fireman on loan to Branksome Depot.

Ivatt Class '2MT' 2-6-0 and 2-6-2T

The tank was an incredible little locomotive and some of them were based at Bournemouth during the last years of steam. Very light on both coal and water with a roomy comfortable cab they were a joy to work on and more than filled the gap left by the withdrawal of the 'M7' class. The rocking grate greatly assisted in the disposal duties of the fireman and ease of lubrication made preparation a clean and simple task for the driver.

The Ivatt '2MT' 2-6-0 was virtually the same as the 2-6-2 tank but had a tender which gave it a much longer range without the need to take water. I never worked on one of these locomotives in my BR days but, fortunately,I have had that pleasure on the Swanage Railway on several occasions during the summer of 1989 and I enjoyed every minute of it.

Class '4MT' 2-6-4T

The ones I worked on were on loan to Bournemouth during a period when the turntable at Weymouth was under repair and their purpose was to work a shuttle service between Bournemouth Central and Weymouth.

The shape of the bunker made it possible to fire on the run when bunker first without being smothered in coal dust. It was a fact that if you held a tissue to the shovelling flap it would be sucked up and out of the top of the bunker.

The cut away bunker did not obstruct the driver's view and these features made them popular with the Southern men who worked on them.

It is not difficult to see why the Standard class locomotives were built very much to the designs of the LMS because they were excellent in every way.

Class '1F' 0-6-0T

I worked on the No. 41708 which is a good little locomotive and has done some really first class work at Swanage but, as trains there are now so much heavier, it is necessary to work her almost beyond her capacity so, unless a lot of repairs are carried out, she will have to be relegated to lighter duties, a great pity but none the less true.

Canadian National 0-8-0 Switchers

Originally built for shunting duties, these locomotives were used in their last years for light freight work when they were replaced by diesel-electrics for shunting. With large cylinders and small wheels, they had a tractive effort well in excess of a 'Merchant Navy' locomotive and, having a large firebox, could be worked hard for long periods.

They were hand fired, having a firehole door almost identical to a 'Merchant' which was an 'Ajax' but worked by air instead of steam. Operated by a treadle, the door was simple to use and very reliable in action, providing it was kept well lubricated. They had large, well protected cabs to cope with Canadian winters.

The SE&CR Locomotives

I worked on three classes of former SE&CR locomotives when Bournemouth men took over the running of the 'Airways' trains from Stewarts Lane crews. Two classes, the 'D' class 4-4-0 'Coppertops' and the 'L' class 4-4-0 'German' engines were used in the early days and proved to be good for the job once we got used to them. The reversing lever was, at times, troublesome being worked by steam, but they were free steaming and had a good turn of speed.

These engines were replaced by 'T9s' which I much preferred as I was well acquainted with them because we had several of them at Bournemouth.

The last of the SECR classes I worked on was an 'O1' class 0-6-0 tender loco and this was on the 'Airways' train also.

The Standard Locomotives

Designed after the Interchange Trials of 1948, these locomotives were, in most cases, very close to the LMS classes and were, for the most part, very efficient but, they had certain points that could have been improved, but almost without exception I liked them all.

'Britannia' Class 4-6-2 (70000s)

I worked on these on a few occasions and I liked them well enough but most of the turns were only over short distances. It would be unfair to venture any form of opinion on that basis but I would not have swapped a 'Merchant Navy' for one of them.

Class '5' 4-6-0 (73000s)

These locomotives were so much like a 'Black Five' that they could have been one and the same except that the '73s' had the advantage of a rocking grate. Free steaming and free running with a top speed well in excess of their top permitted 85 mph limit on the Southern. They rode very well, had a good lookout and were relatively light on coal. In fact, the only fault was one common to all 'Standards' and that was the gap between engine and tender which tended to make the dust fly. This was improved later by the addition of rubber sheeting.

Class '4MT' 2-6-0 (76000s)

I worked on these locomotives more than any other of the Standards and they were equally at home on passenger or freight work. Their only vice was the reversing lever and if you had a lot of shunting to do the effort needed to turn the wheel was tiring and this was an ideal situation to let the fireman have a go at driving! Strong, compact and comfortable, they had a good turn of speed and could handle a train with ease, would steam well and give you a good ride. The ones with the small tenders had a far better lookout when running tender first.

Class '4MT' 4-6-0 (75000s)

These locomotives were rather deceptive because their larger size gave the impression that they must be far superior to the 76000s but, this was not so in practice and the first time I worked on one I almost came to grief on Parkstone Bank.

The load was the same for both of these classes and I had a full load but, instead of making full use of the easier gradient leaving Poole as I would have done with the 76000, I ambled along until I reached the sharper rise, then gave her more power but, I found that I had to give her more lever, then all of the regulator as we lost speed. Dropping the lever over to full I was dismayed to see the speed fall even lower and by now I was of the opinion that we would not even reach Parkstone station.

We were down to walking pace at Parkstone and with the easier grade through the station we gained a little more momentum and struggled on up to the top of the bank. This experience taught me a lesson and that was not to judge by appearances and after that I always made sure to gain all the speed I could before getting into the worst part of the bank, no matter what class of engine I was working on.

These locomotives were pleasant to work on, responding well to the right driving techniques and steaming well at all times, providing a good sloping fire was maintained by the fireman.

Class '3MT' 2-6-2T (82000s)

A very versatile locomotive equally at home on passenger or freight work given a reasonable load. Compact with a good look out and easily accessible controls made them ideal for shunting duties, but with long loose coupled trains care had to be taken with the braking. Having all the advantages of the Standard classes, they made the work so much easier for the fireman and were liked by all who worked on them.

Class '4MT' 2-6-4T (80000s)

With more power than the 82000 class these locomotives were found on all types of trains and were a vast improvement on the older locomotives, especially when bunker first running was involved. The bunker shape cut dust down to the minimum and made for good vision when running in reverse. They could reach the maximum for steam trains of 85 mph but when used on freight trains, as they often were, had a tendency to break their brake blocks which on one occasion gave me cause for concern when descending Parkstone bank with its 1 in 50 gradient. I had a full load with only two vacuum-fitted wagons next to the engine and when I applied the brake showers of sparks came from the trailing driving wheel on my side and the brake was almost useless. However, we had a clear run through Poole Station but our speed was above the limit, although not dangerously so. I managed to stop but well past the ground signal to take us back into the yard.

On examination I found that the rear brake block had broken and had tipped over with the end only coming into contact with the wheel. This prevented the rest of the brake gear from doing its job effectively as well as badly scoring the tyre, making it necessary to have a new tyre fitted at Eastleigh Works.

All of the blocks were in a badly worn condition and cracks were evident in others and a completely new set had to be fitted at Bournemouth before she could be sent up to the Works. The two vacuum-braked wagons, plus a vigilant guard, had helped save the day but, fortunately, I am not one to let such an incident bother me, although it could have been nasty if the signals had been against us.

This did not put me off these locomotives and I look forward to working on them again when the two we have, Nos. 80078 and 80104 are back in service after being restored.

Class '9F' 2-10-0 (92000s)

I worked on these locomotives, including *Evening Star*, on a few occasions and they were the most powerful engines that I encountered on British Railways.

I had one on the 11.13 pm freight from Hamworthy Junction and on arrival at Poole the train was made up to 72 wagons which was equal to a double load for 'King Arthur' or similar engine. We had a banking locomotive which was fitted with a pole reversing lever and slide valves which made it necessary to close the regulator to pull the lever up. We were loose banked as far as Branksome and when we left Poole with this heavy load I gave the '9F' plenty of regulator as we were faced with a 1 in 50 incline and I was very impressed with the way she gathered speed and felt sure that the banker was doing its job well. Glancing back as we approached the distant signal for Parkstone, which was 'off', I was amazed to see the banker about 30 wagon lengths behind us vainly trying to catch us up. But it never did and the '9F' took the whole train up unassisted, with plenty of lever left and some more regulator opening still available.

Never before had I topped the bank with such ease despite the extremely heavy load and the loss of the banker which was supposed to have been essential!

I would have liked to try one out on a fast passenger train with a good load but, unfortunately, the chance never came along but I am sure they would have given a very good performance.

It is a great pity that the Standard class locomotives had not arrived on the scene 20 years earlier, they would have made life a whole lot easier but on second thoughts, not so interesting or so much of a challenge.

Diesel Locomotives

My very first encounter with a diesel electric locomotive was when I was working with Frank Horn in the Top Link on the new Southern Region locomotives Nos. 10201, 10202 and 10203. After a very short and rather sketchy tuition we were working these diesels up to Waterloo from Bournemouth hauling 13 coach trains and we found them to be efficient, but missed the clamour and sway of our 'West Country' and the daily challenge of a job well done!

I hated the smell of diesel fuel and its fumes, being so much more used to the glorious smell of a steam locomotive with its lively personality which seemed to give it a life of its own. I could never regard the diesels as anything more than a box on wheels, however efficient they may be and there is no denying that they certainly were just that. They are no doubt masters of their job and were the logical replacement for steam, but I could never think of them in the same way as our beloved steam locomotives.

Canadian National GM and ALCO Switchers

My first encounter with these switchers was just as brief and uninformed as in the case of the Southern '10201' class, but for some reason I took to these much more readily.

Small by Canadian standards, but very well suited to their purpose, powerful, easy to handle and having a look out which was superb, I soon learned to like them and never ceased to be impressed by their performance.

There was little to choose between the two types, but I preferred the ALCOs; exactly why I am never sure, but they just seemed to have the edge in comfort and pulling power. They made switching, or should I say shunting, a pleasure with none of the little annoyances encountered with steam shunting engines such as injectors suddenly blowing out or wheels slipping or sliding in adverse weather. The short wheel base bogies made them very flexible and gave you a good ride even at a good turn of speed.

Nearly forty years on and these locomotives are very similar to what they were then but greatly increased in power and, no doubt, in comfort as well, whilst still maintaining their familiar shape and size.

204 hp Drewry Locomotive

After a three day training period at Christchurch, I was examined by the locomotive inspector, Jack Evans, and duly passed fit to take charge. As I was the only one on our shift to be trained on the '204', I was asked to cover the duty which was a freight train to Hamworthy Goods shunting then a freight back to Poole yard. As no load had been worked out it was left to me to decide just what load I was prepared to take, and as the train was 28 wagon loads of cement, I decided to take the lot and had not the slightest difficulty in making the gradient out of Hamworthy Junction to Hamworthy Goods. On the return journey from the Junction to Poole, the load was 50 wagons. Again I had no hesitation in taking them and reached Poole with no problems. When the loads were fixed they were well below what I had taken which puzzled me in view of the ease that the '204' had managed the job, but it was not for me to reason why.

These locomotives were excellent for shunting but owing to their light weight they did have a tendency to slip when pulling out a long road of wagons and would often slide when the brake was applied. The mechanical gears had to be treated gently and were somewhat jerky in operation but used sensibly were never really a problem.

They were eventually replaced by 275 hp Ruston & Hornsby locomotives which were diesel electric so the transmission problems were solved but, they were often expected to perform tasks beyond their capacity. We had some at Bournemouth, but they were not in service very long before they were withdrawn. They were more suited to light industrial work and were, in my honest opinion, never man enough for the rigours of heavy shunting.

350 hp '08' and '09' Classes

These were ideally suited to shunting work and were really masters of the job. They had plenty of power, a good brake and, I think, their only drawback was the somewhat limited field of vision, especially when bonnet first and a seat that was far from comfortable. It is a pity that this was not rectified, because, I think, it would have been a whole lot better for those condemned to fill time shunting through no fault of their own. They could pull a good load, but if used on freight trains care was necessary to avoid any danger of overspeeding which meant keeping below 27.5 mph on the '09s' and 15 mph on the '08s'. The resulting brake application and power loss could give the guard a nasty shake up with a loose coupled train.

1550 hp Class '33s'

I had my first full instruction course on these engines, which proved to be a bit of a headache lasting three weeks. We had to learn to drive them; how to check for faults and failures and, after steam locomotives, to understand them was not easy.

So many parts, all of which were completely new to us, had to be remembered and so many points needed to be checked in the event of problems which, fortunately, were few and far between.

Once one got used to the air brake used in conjunction with vacuum brake, the actual driving was not difficult, but we were all very relieved when our course came to an end.

I spent hours of my own time to improve my knowledge of them, a fact that I was never sorry about because on several occasions it did enable me to get out of trouble quickly with the minimum loss of time.

These locomotives became firm favourites of mine and I felt completely at ease.

The cab of was large and extremely comfortable with dual controls positioned within easy reach of the driver, making it possible to drive from either side. Movement from one side of the cab to the other was made simple with the seven second timing delay fitted to the driver's safety device or 'deadman's' (handle) as it is more often called.

Some of these engines were fitted with facilities which made it possible to drive them from a remote cab of a variety of emus, TC units and also a similar class locomotive or an electro diesel.

This locomotive was used successfully for over 20 years on the Bournemouth to Weymouth line and on many other routes. They are now being withdrawn gradually but they must be regarded as one of the best classes of diesel electric to have been in the service of British Rail.

I am sure that all men who have worked on them agree with me on this point and are sorry to witness their demise.

Brush Class '47'

Having a lot more power than the class '33s', these locos were widely used throughout British Rail and formed the backbone of our diesel fleet but, despite this added power I, for one, never felt so much at ease on them as on the smaller diesels.

They were nowhere near as clean to work on, and to walk through the engine was a sure way to get smothered with oil and grease.

Essential switches, such as the brake selector switch, were tucked away in a dark corner making it very difficult to find and operate. The fact that they could only be driven from one side was, at times, a disadvantage and made it necessary to have a second man when shunting was involved.

The failure rate was much higher on these diesels than the '33s' and I, for one, was lucky having only one failure, due to a traction motor fire, during the years I worked on them.

'73' Class Electro Diesel

An electric locomotive fitted with a diesel 600 hp engine for use when away from electrified lines they have proved to be very useful indeed, although more power as an electric locomotive would have made them capable of handling any train on the Southern Region with ease.

Exceptionally clean, comfortable and having plenty of room in the cab, I found them a joy to work on. When worked on electric power they were very quiet and had a first class lookout.

Dual controls made it possible to shunt from both sides of the cab and they could be worked in conjuction with class '33s' or emus on diesel or electric power, including push and pull mode.

They were also useful on trains such as track relaying, ballast or freight, when varying forms of power was called for due to conductor rail isolation.

Owing to their short length, care had to be taken when passing over gaps in the conductor rail so as not to draw an arc from the shoes and this proved to be a problem when these locomotives were first used on the Victoria to Gatwick Airport service.

Modifications were carried out to minimise problems, such as burnt shoe beams and leads, by adding metal shields, and power was cut when the shoes entered a gap to make the camshaft run back so power could build up again when the gap was cleared.

'74' Class Electro Diesel

Powerful, with astonishing acceleration, these locomotives were excellent when all was well but they were, perhaps, the most troublesome locomotives ever on the Southern Region. Constantly breaking down, they were a source of problems for train crews and supervisory staff.

On an early Poole to Waterloo service, I only managed to cover three miles before the locomotive failed and only once during that week did it manage to finish the journey to Waterloo.

These locomotives were converted from electric to electro-diesel by adding a diesel engine of similar power to the '73' class, but of a different make which called for the engine to be run at high revs and in consequence they were very noisy.

We used them on boat trains at Bournemouth to and from Waterloo and I was lucky, except on one occasion when I lost a shoe and the damaged shoe arm caused bad shorting problems which, besides catching fire, kept knocking out the circuit breakers to the conductor rail. After putting out the fire I had to continue on to Eastleigh on diesel power where a replacement locomotive was provided to enable me to complete my journey to Bournemouth.

These locomotives were withdrawn from service early much to everyone's relief and the smaller, but infinitely more reliable, '73' class took over.

Electric Multiple Units

REP Units

Most of my work on these units was done on the REP units which were 3200 hp, 4-car units that could haul two additional 4-car unpowered TC units. Capable of speeds of over 100 mph, these units were restricted to 90 mph to conform with the line speed on the Southern main line.

I had very little trouble during the 20 years that I worked on them. A few broken shoe arms, a broken brake rod, the occasional loss of power, but only once did I fail to complete my journey and on that occasion I had a burnt out traction motor. The unit had to be taken out of service and I was provided with an electro-diesel to complete my journey.

These units were the most powerful on the Southern Region and each of them ran up mileage figures of several million miles. They were in constant use for 20 years before being dismantled to be used in the construction of the new '442' units. The motors were re-used as well as some of the control equipment, having proved so reliable during that period.

The only fault with them was the small cab which was very uncomfortable and badly ventilated. On a run it was impossible to open the side window because of air turbulence set up by the shape of the front end which had a disturbing effect on the ears and could not be endured for more than a few seconds at a time.

When running with only one TC unit attached, it was necessary to coast constantly to avoid over speeding, so good was their acceleration. With the excellent EP brake, one could rapidly reduce speed for a permanent or temporary restriction, then release it to coast at a fraction under that speed. It was easy to use, very positive in action and it was possible to stop on the proverbial sixpence without the slightest difficulty, bringing the train to a halt smoothly with no trace of a jerk.

VEPs and VAD unit No. 8001

The VEPs were 1000 hp 4-car units built for high density work, with plenty of doors to facilitate easy loading and unloading on tight schedules. With a top speed of 90 mph which took longer to obtain than on a REP they had an initial acceleration which was very good, making them ideal for stopping trains. The EP brake was every bit as good as the REPs with precisely the same action.

The VAD unit was a one off, an 8-car unit formed with a 5- car set which had two motor coaches and a 3-car set having one motor coach.

This unit was often combined with 4-car VEP thus giving the train 4000 hp but this proved to be a headache for the electrical controllers as it was prone to knock out the circuit breaker. Great care had to be taken by the driver not to run up the camshaft too quickly thus causing an overload, but this was not always possible. However, if the controller was informed that this unit was in service, he quickly reset the breakers not waiting for notification as to the cause.

Working this formation to Waterloo one day I was stopped at the last signal before entering the station. When the signal was cleared I opened the controller to notch one, moving forward slowly when the leading shoe on my side went into a gap and immediately there was a blinding flash, a loud report and a cloud of acrid yellow smoke issuing from the shoe fuse box. Fragments of metal were hurled across the track striking the bridge alongside the signal box, bringing the signalman to the window to ascertain the cause. The circuit breakers tripped instantly, but were reset without delay and I again slowly opened the controller and was gratified that the unit took power enabling me to run into the station.

On arrival, I was met by the motive power inspector and a fitter who had seen and heard the 'explosion' and they wanted to know what had caused it. I told them 'All I know is that I have lost the leading shoe fuse, but precisely why is a mystery to me!' I went on to explain that I had only opened up to notch one to dispel any thought they may have had to the contrary.

They went around the whole train but could find no other fuse that had been affected but, examination of the leading shoe fuse box showed that the entire fuse had literally blown to pieces badly scoring and burning the inside of the box.

The securing bolts had melted to immoveable blobs and it was not possible to replace the fuse, but the fitter said that the unit was fit to return to Bournemouth where a new box and lead would be fitted.

My relief driver, Bill Noel, arrived just as they were leaving, so I explained the situation to him and assured him that the fitter had cleared the unit, but jokingly said, 'You will probably progressively lose your shoe fuses on the way down'.

The next day he relieved me and said 'I was expecting trouble all the way on my trip down yesterday but didn't get any'. I said I was sorry, explaining that I was only pulling his leg, but realised that I should not have done so because he accepted my word without question.

These units were eventually split up to be incorporated into new VEPs.

CIGs and BIGs

Similar to the VEP but with less doors and seats, they were more comfortable for passengers and were mainly used on the Portsmouth route. The power and braking was the same as the VEPs.

CEPs and BEPs

These units were mostly on the Kent coast run, but did stray over onto the Western section at times and in later years they have been refurbished, to include a public address system. The brake valve was of the older five position type but still EP and, if anything, were slightly more difficult to bring to a smooth halt, but after a few stops this was overcome.

If for any reason the EP brake could not be used the auto brake had to be applied but it was very positive in action and would bring a train quickly to a halt.

HAP and SAP Units

I did a lot of work on these units in the early days of the Bournemouth electrification and I felt quite at ease with them. Their open cab gave them a more spacious feel, the brakes were good and controlled by a five position handle for either EP or auto brake application.

Ventilation was much better on these units than the corridor fitted ones as the air could flow smoothly round the curved front without causing the disagreeable effect found on the REPs etc.

The 'Nelsons'

These units were nicknamed 'Nelsons' because they only had one window in the front and they were long associated with the Portsmouth line. Fitted with the Westinghouse brake, they had to be braked carefully when formed of 12 cars as they were prone to 'snatching' but, in general, they were well liked by the men who worked on them regularly.

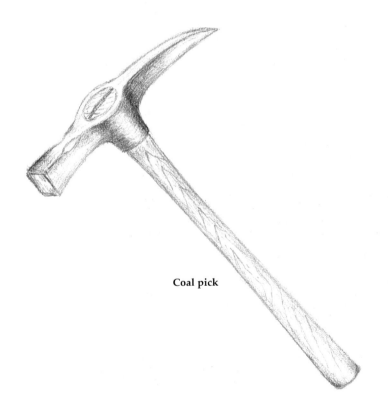

Coal pick

Appendix Two

Locomotive Equipment

All steam locomotives were equipped with essential tools for everyday use and these were kept in lockers or steel boxes at various locations on each engine.

Throughout the years, several different methods were used to make them secure, the most usual was by using padlocks, but keys were often mislaid or taken home by mistake, making it necessary to force open the locks with disastrous results.

Another answer was to take all the hand tools to the stores at the end of each day, which meant carrying them from the disposal pit to the shed, an arduous task likely to be conveniently forgotten and doomed to failure.

Finally, all tools were left on the engines and they tended to disappear, making it necessary to take the required tools from locomotives that were in the shed for washout or repairs.

Standard equipment on all Southern engines was as follows:

12 detonators in metal container	4 headlamps
2 red flags	4 disc boards.
1 handlamp	Wire and worsted for making trimmings
1 oil feeder	Gauge glasses and rubber rings
1 thick pot for cylinder oil	string asbestos
1 bucket	2 flare lamps
1 handbrush	1 gauge glass lamp
1 hammer	A variety of ring and open end spanners.
1 coalpick	A set of fire irons consisting of clinker shovel,
1 pin punch	pricker and dart

On locomotives with long fireboxes, extra fire irons were necessary so double the number were carried. The 'Schools' and 'Lord Nelsons' classes also carried a special tool to open the steam cocks on the footplate.

Last, but not least, was, of course, the firing shovel, which was without doubt the most used tool of the lot. The shovel to the fireman was as important as the trowel is to a bricklayer and, used skilfully, could be the means of making the job so much easier and so much more rewarding when the engine was responding to it.

A good fireman made sure that all the tools were in tip-top condition by removing burrs, cleaning, straightening and replacing when necessary. Nothing was worse than to find a locomotive with a bad set of tools because the job was made so much more difficult than it need be.

Some drivers carried a small tin in their bag with an assortment of their own tools to make various jobs, such as replacing trimmings or changing a gauge glass, so much easier. A pair of pliers, a knife, a special square spanner for gauge glass tops, an assortment of plug and tail trimmings, some corks and other odds and ends, all made the difference to the ease in doing a quick repair or replacement.

One other item carried by a few men, especially those who attended First Aid classes, was a small tin containing a matchstick to which was fixed a loop of fine horsehair and this was used to remove small particles of ash that often got into your eyes with very painful results.

A firm in Grimsby used to make a tin box for train crews and these were very popular. They came in a variety of sizes and were strong, with a section in the lid for time books, wrong line orders, rule book and driver's tickets.

I had a fireman booked with me one day and he was carrying a brand new one, resplendent with its brass handle and name plate and the first part of our duty was to ride passenger to Poole and relieve the crew on 'Q' class locomotive No. 548, then do a short spell of shunting. On arrival there I asked the fireman, Johnny Long, if he would like to have a go at the controls while we were shunting. He readily agreed to do so, and instead of putting his box in the locker he slid it under the steam reverser cover plate out of the way then sat down on the driver's side seat.

The shunter, who was ready to start work, asked him to set back on to some wagons, so he pulled the reverser into back gear and there was an ominous crunch from under the metal plate. We looked in horror in that corner and our fears were well founded because the box was under the crank of the reverser powered by 200 lb. of steam pressure.

Gently placing the reverser into forward gear released the box, but it was now a sorry sight with the lid section almost flat and one side crumpled to about half of its original height. The contents were in a real mess, the milk bottle having broken, flooding John's sandwiches as well as the towel he carried.

We emptied the contents and while John did the shunting I set to work on the box and succeeded in getting it back into a reasonable shape, but that certainly dispelled any thoughts I had of buying one.

The last item of personal equipment was the tea can, which was introduced to men on the South Western section by men moving into it from the South Eastern section for the purpose of promotion. Before that time most South Western men carried a bottle of tea, which was often drunk cold but, some men chose to warm it by placing the bottle in the dish above the firehole door and the square type Johnny Walker's whisky bottle was sought after because it did not move about.

By using the tea can the men could have a fresh cup of tea when they needed it as boiling water was available at numerous points and both men took it in turn to supply the ingredients, but it was usually the fireman who made it.

A few words must be written about the use of headlights and disc boards, as used on the Southern because this railway was different from the rest in the fact that headcodes used were to indicate the route of trains, lamps by night and disc boards by day. All other railways used only lamps and these were used to show the type of train.

Southern disc boards also carried duty numbers. For example, the up 'Royal Wessex' was 381 duty and this enabled signalmen and loco. supervisors to readily identify the train or locomotive.

Every headlamp was fitted with red slides to turn it into a tail lamp when required. The square type had flat metal framed slides and the round type had curved glass that fitted into the revolving centre part of the lamp. These lamps were filled with paraffin but some locomotives, such as 'Merchant Navy' class, 'West Country' and 'Battle of Britain' classes were fitted with a steam powered generator and this provided electric current for the headlights, plus illumination for the footplate and its gauges. Some other engines that were converted to oil fired were also fitted with steam generators and retained them when the locomotives again reverted back to coal fired.

Appendix Three

Train Timings

I have included some time tables dating back to the 1952 period when steam was at its peak on the Southern, comparing them with 1991 times over the same routes. The differences are quite remarkable. In 1952 there were, of course, more restrictions of speed and I quote those for the Southern Region.

Inside Suburban Area:
Steam trains must not exceed a maximum speed of 60 miles per hour at any point and all restrictions which impose lower speeds than 60 m.p.h must be observed.
The Suburban Area for the purpose of this instruction is all routes between

London and Dartford
London and Hither Green
London and St Mary Cray Junction via Bickley
London and South Croydon Junction
London and Leatherhead Junction
Waterloo and Malden
Waterloo and Feltham Junction

Outside Surburban Area:
Steam Trains - Must not exceed a maximum speed of 85 miles per hour at any point and all restrictions that impose lower speeds than 85 mph must be strictly observed.
Making up time (Steam Trains) when passenger trains are running late, drivers must endeavour to make up time, both inside and outside the Suburban area, but all speed restrictions must be complied with.

There have been lots of changes in recent years and the speed limits are as now follows on the Waterloo to Weymouth line.

Waterloo to Clapham Junction	60 mph	
Clapham Junction to New Malden	75 mph	Through line
Clapham Junction to New Malden	60 mph	Local lines
New Malden to Bournemouth	90 mph	
Farnborough to Eastleigh	100 mph	'442' units only
Bournemouth to Weymouth	85 mph	

Slower speeds apply at
Swaythling	75 mph
Northam Jn.	25 mph
Southampton Tunnel	40 mph
Brockenhurst	80 mph
Christchurch	60 mph

And at various other points to Weymouth.

The times below show comparison between steam and electric journeys.

Fast Steam Time	Waterloo to Weymouth	3 hours 20 minutes
Fast Electric Time	Waterloo to Weymouth	2 hours 30 minutes

(Steam train stopping 8 times; electric train stopping 11 times, 50 minutes faster)

Semi-fast Steam Time	Waterloo to Bournemouth	2 hours 52 minutes
Semi-fast Electric Time	Waterloo to Bournemouth	2 hours 2 minutes

(Steam train stopping 11 times; electric train stopping 13 times; 50 minutes faster)

Fast Steam Time   Waterloo to Bournemouth   2 hours 11 mins
Fast Electric Time   Waterloo to Bournemouth   1 hours 35½ mins
(Steam train with only one intermediate stop; electric train with three intermediate stops is 35½ minutes faster.)

The above tables give a clear indication of the improvement in timings achieved by electric multiple units. Speed, comfort, heating, and lighting is today vastly superior to that provided in steam days. Of that there is no question but when it comes to reliability then that is questionable.

During 28½ years of working on steam only twice was it necessary to have a change of locomotive, both times through brake failures. This total was multiplied many times over, with three failures occuring in one day for various reasons, during 20 years of working on diesel and electric powered trains.

Steam Trains from/to Waterloo

	Arr.		Dep.
Waterloo			15.20
Worting Jn		16.14	
Winchester City	16.34		16.36
Southampton Central	16.53		16.58
Brockenhurst	17.17		17.19
Bournemouth Central	17.40		
Waterloo			15.30
Basingstoke	16.31		16.34
Micheldever	16.51		16.52
Winchester City	17.03		17.05
Southampton Central	17.26		17.31
Brockenhurst	17.50		17.53
New Milton	18.03		18.05
Christchurch	18.13		18.15
Pokesdown	18.20		18.22
Bournemouth Central	18.22		
'The Royal Wessex'			
Waterloo			16.35
Worting Jn		17.30	
Winchester City	17.49		17.51
Southampton Central	18.08		18.12
Brockenhurst	18.31		18.34
Bournemouth Central	18.55		18.59
Poole	19.09		19.11
Wareham	19.21		19.24
Dorchester South	19.42		19.44
Weymouth	19.55		
Waterloo			18.30
Worting Jn		19.26	
Southampton Central	20.01		20.05
Bournemouth Central	20.41		
'The Royal Wessex'			
Weymouth			07.34
Dorchester South	07.48½		07.49½
Wool	08.01		08.02
Wareham	08.09½		08.14½
Poole	08.24½		08.25½
Bournemouth Central	08.35		08.40
Southampton Central	09.13		09.16½
Winchester City	09.36½		09.38
Worting Jn		10.01	
Waterloo	10.50		

11.30 Weymouth to Waterloo (Abbreviated)

	Arr.		Dep.
Weymouth			11.30
Bournemouth Central	12.35		12.40
Southampton Central	13.15		13.20
Worting Jn		13.59	
Waterloo	14.49		

13.25 Weymouth to Waterloo (Abbreviated)

Weymouth			13.35
Bournemouth Central	14.35		14.40
Southampton Central	15.14		15.20
Worting Jn		15.59	
Waterloo	16.52		

Current Electric Multiple '442' Unit Timings
Down trains from Waterloo to Weymouth / Poole.

	(Fast)		
Waterloo			11.32
Worting Jn		12.13	
Southampton Parkway (Airport)	12.30		12.31
Southampton	12.37½		12.39½
Brockenhurst	12.52½		12.53½
Bournemouth	13.07½		13.11½
Poole	13.20		13.21½
Wareham	13.31		13.32
Wool	13.38		13.39
Moreton	13.43		13.44
Dorchester South	13.50		13.52
Upwey	13.57		13.58
Weymouth	14.08		

	(Semi-fast)	
Waterloo		11.45
Clapham Jn	11.52	11.52½
Woking	12.05½	12.07½
Basingstoke	12.29½	12.31
Winchester	12.46	12.47
Eastleigh	12.55	12.56
Southampton Parkway (Airport)	12.59	13.00
Southampton	13.06½	13.09½
Totton	13.14	13.14½
Brockenhurst	13.24	13.25
New Milton	13.31½	13.32½
Christchurch	13.38½	13.39½
Pokesdown	13.43	13.43½
Bournemouth	13.47	13.51
Branksome	13.54½	13.55½
Parkstone	13.57½	13.58½
Poole	14.02	

Appendix Four

Canadian National Railway Rules

As a matter of interest I have listed some of the rules from the Canadian National Rulebook of 1952 that I found so different from ours.

Rule 454

Where a 'stop and proceed' signal is used as a station protection signal, trains or engines affected by it must stop before reaching the signal and not more than 100 yards from it and may then proceed at yard speed expecting to find the track occupied, switch not properly lined, broken rail or other obstruction and preceded by a flagman when necessary to ensure complete protection.

Rule 509A

When a train or engine approaches a 'stop and proceed' signal indicating stop it must, except as prescribed by rule 509B stop before reaching the signal and not more than 100 yards from it and may then proceed at once at restricted speed.

Rule 509B

Where authorised a 'stop and proceed' block signal may be designated as a grade signal. A train handling 50 per cent or more of ruling grade tonnage approaching a grade signal indicating stop may pass it without stopping and proceed at restricted speed to the next signal. A grade signal will be designated by a yellow marker attached to the mast showing the letter 'G'.

Engineer's cap

Appendix Five

The First 100 Locomotives and Multiple Units

On 8th December, 1991 at Swanage station, I was presented with an engraved plaque to commemorate the fact that I had worked on the footplate of 100 types of traction. With my continued activity at Swanage this total has continued to increase. The first 100 types are listed below.

Steam

LSWR Adams 'T1' class 0-4-4T
LSWR Adams '02' class 0-4-4T
LSWR Adams 'T3' class 4-4-0 'Highflyer'
LSWR Drummond '700' class 0-6-0 'Black Motor'
LSWR Drummond 'T9' class 4-4-0 'Greyhound'
LSWR Drummond 'M7' class 0-4-4T 'Motor Tank'
LSWR Drummond 'D15' class 4-4-0
LSWR Drummond 'T14' class 4-6-0 'Paddleboat'
LSWR Drummond 'K10' class 4-4-0 'Small Hopper'
LSWR Drummond 'L11' class 4-4-0 'Big Hopper'
LSWR Drummond 'L12' class 4-4-0 'Bulldog'
LSWR Adams 'A12' class 0-4-2T 'Jubilee'
LSWR/SR Urie and Maunsell 'H15' class 4-6-0
LSWR/SR Urie and Maunsell 'S15' class 4-6-0
LSWR Urie 'H16' class 4-6-2T
LSWR Urie 'N15' 'King Arthur' class 4-6-0
SR Maunsell 'N15' 'King Arthur' class 4-6-0 'Eastleigh Arthurs'
SR Maunsell 'N15' 'King Arthur' class 4-6-0 'Scotch Arthurs'
SR Maunsell 'Schools' 'V' class 4-4-0
SR Maunsell 'Lord Nelson' class 4-6-0
SR Maunsell 'U' class 2-6-0 'U-Boats'
SR Maunsell 'U1' class 2-6-0 'U-Boats'
SECR Maunsell 'N' class 2-6-0
SECR Maunsell 'N1' class 2-6-0
SR Maunsell 'Q' class 0-6-0
SR Bulleid 'Q1' class 0-6-0 'Charlies'
SR Bulleid 'Merchant Navy' class 4-6-2 'Packets'
SR Bulleid 'Battle of Britain' class 4-6-2 'Spam Cans'
SR Bulleid 'West Country' class 4-6-2 'Spam Cans'
SR Maunsell 'N15X' 'Remembrance' class 4-6-0
LBSC Marsh 'H1' class 4-4-2 'Brighton Atlantics'
LBSC Marsh 'H2' 4-4-2 'Brighton Atlantics'
LBSC Stroudley 'A1X' class 0-6-0T 'Terriers'
LBSC Billinton 'K' class 2-6-0 'Moguls'
SECR Wainwright 'D' class 4-4-0 'Coppertops'
SECR Wainwright 'L' class 4-4-0 'German Engines'
SECR Wainwright 'O1' class 0-6-0
LSWR Adams 'B4' class 0-4-0T 'The Bug'
LSWR Drummond 'G6' class 0-6-0T 'Yard Shunter'
USA 'S.160' class 2-8-0
USA 0-6-0T

Ministry of Supply Riddles 'WD' 'Austerity' class 2-8-0
GWR Churchward '43XX' class 2-6-0
GWR Collett '51XX' class 2-6-2T 'Prairies'
GWR Collett '57XX' class 0-6-0T 'Panniers'
GWR Collett '49XX' 'Hall' class 4-6-0
GWR Collett '68XX' 'Grange' class 4-6-0
GWR Collett '56XX' class 0-6-2T
LMS Stanier '5MT' class 4-6-0 'Black Fives'
LMS Stanier '8F' class 2-8-0
MR Johnson '1F' class 0-6-0T
LMS Fowler '2P' class 4-4-0
LMS Fowler '4F' class 0-6-0
LMS Ivatt '2MT' class 2-6-0
LMS Ivatt '2MT' class 2-6-2T 'Mickey Mouse'
LMS Fowler/Stanier/Fairburn '4MT' class 2-6-4T
LMS Fowler '3F' class 0-6-0T 'Jinty'
LNER Gresley 'V2' class 2-6-2
LNER Gresley 'A4' class 4-6-2
LNER Gresley 'N7' class 0-6-2T
NER Worsdell 'J72' class 0-6-0T
BR Riddles '7MT' 'Britannia' class 4-6-2
BR Riddles '5MT' '73XXX' class 4-6-0
BR Riddles '4MT' '75XXX' class 4-6-0
BR Riddles '4MT' '76XXX' class 2-6-0
BR Riddles '4MT' '80XXX' class 2-6-4T
BR Riddles '3MT' '82XXX' class 2-6-2T
BR Riddles '9F' class 2-10-0
CNR 0-8-0 'Switcher'
Hunslet No. 1690 *Cunarder* 0-6-0ST
Hunslet No. 3694 *Whiston* 0-6-0ST
Hudswell Clarke No. 1704 *Nunlow* 0-6-0T
Hawthorn Leslie No. 3931 'No. 21' 0-6-0T

Diesel

English Electric '08' and '09' classes 0-6-0
Birmingham RC&W Type '3' class '33' Bo-Bo 'Cromptons'
Brush Type '4' class '47' Co-Co
Drewry '04' class 0-6-0 '204s'
Ruston & Hornsby '07' class 0-6-0
CNR Alco 1000 hp 'Switcher'
CNR GM 900 hp 'Switcher'
LMS No. 10000 Co-Co
No. 10201 1Co-Co1

Electro-Diesel

BR class '73' 'ED'
English Electric class '73/1' 'ED'
BR class '74' 'Big ED'

EMUs

4-REP
4-VEP
4-CIG

4-BIG
4-CEP
4-BEP
4-HAP
4-SAP
VAB
EPB 1951
EPB 1957
4-SUB
'Nutcrackers'
De-Icer

DMUs

2 x 550 hp 'Hastings Units'